PRAYING FOR OUR CHILDREN

120 Prayers From A Father's Heart

Apostle Dr. Eddie Maestas

Dominion Unlimited Publications

PRAYING FOR OUR CHILDREN

Apostle Dr. Eddie Maestas

Copyright © 2023 Apostle Dr. Eddie Maestas

Praying For Our Children: 120 Prayers From A Father's Heart. Copyright 2021-2023 Apostle, Dr. Eddie Maestas
Print ISBN: 979-8-9859944-5-2
E-Book ISBN Kindle: 979-8-9872129-0-5
Cover design by Jennifer Foster.
Unless otherwise indicated, all scripture quotations are taken from the New King James Version of the Bible. Scriptures marked NKJV are taken from the NEW KING JAMES VERSION (NKJV): Scripture taken from the NEW KING JAMES VERSION®.
Copyright© 1982 by Thomas Nelson, Inc. Used by permission. All rights reserved
Scripture quotations marked (AMPC) are taken from the Amplified® Bible. Copyright © 1954, 1958, 1962, 1964, 1965, 1987 by The Lockman Foundation. Used by permission.
Scripture quotations marked (MSG) are taken from The Message, copyright © 1993, 2002, 2018 by Eugene H. Peterson. Used by permission of NavPress. All rights reserved. Represented by Tyndale House Publishers, Inc.
Scripture quotations marked (NKJV) are taken from the New King James Version®. Copyright © 1982 by Thomas Nelson. Used by permission. All rights reserved.
Scripture quotations marked (TLB) are taken from The Living Bible copyright © 1971. Used by permission of Tyndale House Publishers, Inc., Carol Stream, Illinois 60188. All rights reserved.
Scripture quotations marked (TPT) are from The Passion Translation®. Copyright © 2017, 2018 by Passion & Fire Ministries, Inc. Used by permission. All rights reserved. ThePassionTranslation.com.
All rights reserved. Printed in the United States of America.

To my wife Araceli, my mom, Helen Ortiz, and my family. Jacob & Rachelle; Tom & Nicolette; Eddie, Micah, Noah, & Hailey; Lucas, Adrian & Jessica. To Anthony & Amanda; Gabriel & Vanessa. To our grandkids, Kalila, Sophie, Faith, Liam, Caleb, Ezekiel, Dainty, Siena, Graydon, Silas, and Kingston. We love you all very much and we declare all of our family shall be saved and will fulfill their God-given purpose.

This book is dedicated first of all to my wife Araceli Maestas, the woman I love who has helped me to become a better person.

Thank you for being a blessing to me and to all our kids and grandkids, who we love very much. Thank you for never giving up on us while God was still changing us.

We have a desire for all parents and grandparents to see their kids protected and to fulfill their God-given purpose in this world. We know that there are many things of darkness and deception that are always trying to take our kids captive. But we believe the best thing we can do to help and cover our kids comes through our prayers of intercession.

I also dedicate this book to my mom, Pastor Helen Ortiz. My mom prayed for me and stood in the gap for many years when I was living a very dark life. I know it's because of her prayers that God's mercy covered me until I* woke up and surrendered my life to Christ. Thanks, Mom. I love you very much and thank you for being the woman of God you are. A woman that has never given up or compromised Your faith.

Also to my kids. I am sorry for the times I was not the best kind of father, or even an example of who our Lord really wanted me to be. But one thing II never did was to stop loving you and praying for you. I did not know how to be a good man or a good father. I was so caught up on my hurts and strongholds, which caused me to not be a very good father to you for many years; but Christ was being formed in me, and I never gave up because of my love for you, my children, and my God. He has truly been merciful to me and us and has always blessed me more than I have ever deserved.

Thank You, Father. Because of the work You started in me and our kids, You will complete it until Christ is fully formed in us.

CONTENTS

Title Page
Praying for Our Children
Copyright
Dedication
Foreword
A Simple Thanks
Prophetic Prayers For Our Children   1
The Birthing Season   2
Part One   4
The Kingdom Of God   19
A Word To Parents   34
Part Two   40
Exhortation for Parents   46
Exhortation   56
A Movement   67
Part Three   68
Relationship Building   78
Prayer For The Weary   88
Part Four   94
The Corporate Body   100
We Have Access   111

Finally, My Brethren	123
Afterword	125

FOREWORD

Hello Family.

You are entering into a 120-day prayer journey, a journey filled with the prayers of intercession and petitions for the future destiny of our children and the generations of children to come.

Apostle Eddie, known to many as Papa Eddie, was moved by the Spirit of God to embark on a season of dedicated prayer and declaration for 120 days. Apostle Eddie carries a strong burden of the Lord concerning his children, our children, and the children all over the world that do not know the Lord.

Each prayer targets specific areas of need and concerns, as well as the tremendous challenges that our youth face today. For 120 days, Apostle Eddie along with a company of believers prayed. Many interventions took place in the lives of many children and families. It is not too late. Join in and gain the benefit of these powerful prayers which are in a book format so that each believer can prayer along until the breakthrough begins to happen.

> [One] generation passed away, and [another] generation cometh: but the earth abided forever. Ecclesiastes 1:4 KJV

Apostle Eddie is a man after the heart of God. On many occasions I heard him cry out of a broken heart for the body of Christ and those who are lost in this world. I believe God has given Apostle Eddie a deep desire and passion to see the love of God spread throughout the entire world, one person at a time.

And I thank God I have been asked to be a part of that journey. God has enlarged His tent pegs, and His Love and Unity is spreading like wildfire throughout the nations.

The number 120 signifies the passing away of the age of the flesh, and the beginning of the age of the Spirit.

[2]I will open my mouth in a parable: I will utter dark sayings of old: [3]Which we have heard and known, and our fathers have told us. [4]We will not hide [them] from their children, shewing to the generation to come the praises of the LORD, and his strength, and his wonderful works that he hath done. [5]For he established a testimony in Jacob, and appointed a law in Israel, which he commanded our fathers, that they should make them known to their children: [6]That the generation to come might know [them, even] the children [which] should be born; [who] should arise and declare [them] to their children: [Psalm 78:2-6 KJV]

Big Love
Apostle Calvin Cook
Golden Altar Ministries
San Jose, California USA

A SIMPLE THANKS

Scrolling through social media pages one day, I came across a bold declaration, *"I'm going to pray for our kids..."* These words are so aligned with the heart of God.

My spiritual father, Apostle Dr. Eddie Maestas made this statement. Not a lot of fanfare, just one simple statement. But the impact has been tremendous.

He did not release the 120 prayers daily, but near enough that they became anchors for the souls of many of his online followers. In fact, it inspired a few of them to share the God-given prayers that they released. It's so exciting to witness the power of God as the hearts of the fathers increasingly call to their children.

Within each prayer are seeds of hope, gratitude, inspiration, and instruction. *"Don't give up. Keep trusting God. Expect the miraculous."*

And that's precisely what has occurred. Prodigals, called out of the mindsets of orphans and vagabonds, are returning home. Hearts are mending. Restoration. Reparation. Repentance. Healing. Love. Unity. The power of God is victorious through these simple prayers.

And so, we've compiled them here, in a slightly longer form, with scriptures and apostolic prophetic exhortations. As a spiritual son, I say, *"Thank you, Papa Eddie. We needed this."*

As a mother and a minister, I stand alongside of you with the same proclamation, *"We're going to keep praying for our kids. We will prophesy, decree, declare, and expect the impossible with man to manifest through God."*

It began with a prophetic cry from the Father's heart. A cry that required His son Eddie's spiritual response. Listen. Prophesy. Speak the words. Create the atmosphere. Let the children come to Me. Amen. It is so. He who has ears to hear, let him listen. And hear.

Lonzine Lee, Pastor/Teacher
Astounding Love! A Global Church Fellowship and Training Center
Principal, Dominion Unlimited Publications
Manteca, California USA

PROPHETIC PRAYERS FOR OUR CHILDREN

Why do we pray over our children prophetically?

We all have been given the gift of prophecy, not just to give a word to someone, but to have spiritual discernment and insight, and to speak the same words over our lives that our Father has spoken over us.

What we see is not given so we can worry, but so we can pray and make intercession for our family and friends. We pray forth what God wants us to speak forth into the future of our children to have wisdom and the knowledge of God for any situation.

We can see things as the Spirit of God reveals them to us prophetically. That is how I pray over my children and see things before they even happen. We need to be in front of every situation, praying a God given word over our kids as we see things by the Spirit.

What we speak becomes a word unto our children. The enemy has to bow to what we speak. This will bring our kids into alignment with the word and into their God given destiny.

Pursue love, and desire spiritual gifts, but especially that you may prophesy. 1Corinthians 14:1

THE BIRTHING SEASON

The idea of releasing these daily prayers for our children was birthed while I was going through a very difficult time with a couple of my own kids. The Lord told me to take time to travail, not just for my own children, but for all the parents that were facing similar things with their sons and daughters. I would sit before the Lord and not know what to pray. All I saw was many, many parents all going through hard times with their children.

This world has really influenced so many kids with the things of this world.

So, I began to pray according to Romans 8:26-28, where it's written that The Holy Spirit helps us in our weaknesses. That when we don't know what to pray on our own, the Spirit will help us pray. And I began to experience the Spirit showing me what was attacking or hindering our children every day.

Then, as the Spirit led me, I would speak those things in prayers on Facebook for all the parents to pray along with me. Some prayers were along the same lines, because the Lord told me to hit some of the same things over and over again. I would pray in the Spirit for long periods of time until the Holy Spirit gave me what to pray for on that day.

I was hearing testimonies daily on how these prayers were changing their kids. Some were coming back to the Lord, and some had stopped doing the things they were doing. Many parents were experiencing God healing their relationships with their kids, and many were being healed of their wounds, fears, and worries. We must daily fight against the deceptions that try to deceive our children to bring destruction to their lives.

So, I hope these Spirit-led prayers will help you as parents and set our kids free, and that they continue to put a hedge of protection around our children. These prayers will deliver those children who may be bound at this time. We believe that they will come into their God-destined purpose. If your children are doing great, then pray for other children and still keep the hedge of protection everyday over your children.

As a parent I know how a parent can hurt and feel so discouraged and fearful. I went through some very painful times where I thought I was going to lose my children. But I kept fighting the good fight of faith. And it's our faith in God that will cause us to overcome in this world.

PART ONE

Behold, children are a heritage from the LORD, The fruit of the womb is a reward. Like arrows in the hand of a warrior, So are the children of one's youth. Happy is the man who has his quiver full of them; They shall not be ashamed, But shall speak with their enemies in the gate.

Psalm 127:3-5

Declaration - Prayer 1

Let's begin to pray together, taking one minute in the course of our day to pray for our children. Just say *Amen*, that you are in agreement, and we will break the deceiver's influence off of our kids.

We pray that our kids, no matter how old they are, will find their purpose and destiny in God, and that their eyes will be opened to His Kingdom.

We agree that no weapon formed against them will prosper. They are covered in mercy and grace, even while they may presently be lost. Amen.

Now let's take one minute to pray in the Spirit to seal this prayer for our kids. Then we say "Amen," in agreement that it is done.

> No weapon formed against you shall prosper, And every tongue which rises against you in judgment You shall condemn. This is the heritage of the servants of the LORD, And their righteousness is from Me," says the LORD. Isaiah 54:17

Prophetic Decree - Prayer 2

As we pray in the Spirit lifting up our sons, daughters, and grandchildren to the Lord, we bring forth the will of God into the lives of those we are praying for.

Praying in the Spirit, we receive from the Lord what we need to pray. So right now, we release the will of God into their lives. We break any influence that is outside of the will of God for our offspring. We break every foolish decision out of fleshly desires to be broken now in Jesus' Name. Your Kingdom come, Lord and Your will be done in our children's lives.

Now let's take one minute to pray in the Spirit to seal this prayer for our kids. Then we say "Amen," in agreement that it is done.

> Let Your work appears to Your servants, And Your glory to their children. Psalm 90:6

> Then little children were brought to Him that He might put His hands on them and pray, but the disciples rebuked them. 14But Jesus said, "Let the little children come to Me, and do not forbid them; for of such is the kingdom of heaven." Matthew 19:13-14

> Likewise the Spirit also helps in our weaknesses. For we do not know what we should pray for as we ought, but the Spirit Himself makes intercession for us with groanings which cannot be uttered. Now He who searches the hearts knows what the mind of the Spirit is, because He makes intercession for the saints according to the will of God. And we know that all things work together for good to those who love God, to those who are the called according to His purpose. Romans 8:26-28

Prophetic Call Into Light - Prayer 3

We call forth this next generation into God's purpose in the earth. No weapon formed against them shall prosper.

We call them healed and delivered from mental deception, anxiety, fear, and captivity – from darkness and its influences. We speak the anointing of God over their minds, and we break every stronghold of bondage holding our children in any form of darkness.

We release Your Light to shine on the lies and deceptions of the enemy and for every deception to be made evident by the Light. We call our children blessed.

Now let's take one minute to pray in the Spirit to seal this

prayer for our children, and grandchildren, and the children and grandchildren of others. Then we say "Amen," in agreement that it is done.

> All Your children shall be taught by the LORD, and great shall be the peace of Your children. Isaiah 54:13

> The righteous man walks in his integrity; blessed (happy, fortunate, enviable) are his children after him. Proverbs 20:7

> But the mercy of the LORD is from everlasting to everlasting on those who fear Him, And His righteousness to children's children, To such as keep His covenant, And to those who remember His commandments to do them. The LORD has established His throne in heaven, And His kingdom rules overall. Psalm 103:17-19

> For he who speaks in a tongue does not speak to men but to God, for no one understands him; however, in the spirit he speaks mysteries. 1Corinthians 14:2

Release Of Divine Purpose - Prayer 4

We must break hell's assignments against our children and grandchildren. We must travail in prayer until Christ be formed in our children and they be brought into God's divine purpose for their lives.

Father, we lift our children unto You. We know You have put a divine purpose within them. We call for Your purpose to be fulfilled in their lives.

We cover our children with Your glory and consecrate them with the anointing unto Yourself, Lord. They are Yours. No false influence can separate them from Your love and desires for their lives. We call them into a transformed life so that they will come into the image and likeness of the Lord so that they will be transformed by the renewing of their minds.

Now let's take one minute to pray in the Spirit to seal this prayer for our kids. Then we say "Amen," in agreement that it is done.

His descendants will be mighty on earth; The generation of the upright will be blessed. Psalm 112:2

The righteous man walks in his integrity; His children are blessed after him. Proverbs 20:7

Let no one deceive himself. If anyone among you seems to be wise in this age, let him become a fool that he may become wise. 1Corinthians 3:18

I beseech you therefore, brethren, by the mercies of God, that you present Your bodies a living sacrifice, holy, acceptable to God, which is Your reasonable service. And do not be conformed to this world, but be transformed by the renewing of Your mind, that you may prove what is that good and acceptable and perfect will of God. For I say, through the grace given to me, to everyone who is among you, not to think of himself more highly than he ought to think, but to think soberly, as God has dealt to each one a measure of faith. Romans 12:1-3

And at the end of the time I, Nebuchadnezzar, lifted my eyes to heaven, and my understanding returned to me; and I blessed the Most High and praised and honored Him…Who lives forever: For His dominion is an everlasting dominion, And His kingdom is from generation to generation. Daniel 4:34

I write to you, fathers, because you have known Him who is from the beginning. I write to you, young men, because you have overcome the wicked one. I write to you, little children, because you have known the Father. 1John 2:13

So, they said, "Believe on the Lord Jesus Christ, and you will be saved, you and Your household." Acts 16:31

Now I say that Jesus Christ has become a servant to the circumcision for the truth of God, to confirm the promises made to the fathers, Romans 15:8

Calling Forth Destiny - Prayer 5

When we pray for our kids and grandchildren, we don't call out the things they are doing wrong or in bondage to. We free them from things of the past, and we call them forward into the perfect will of God. We speak the word of God over them, which is the sword of the Spirit.

Father, we send Your Word to them for it is Your word that heals them spirit, soul, and body. We speak faith, hope and love over our children and grandchildren, and we declare they are covered in mercy and grace.

Lord, we release all Your promises according to Your Word over our children. They are blessed and will live good, long and satisfying lives. We send to them the word of grace and truth and let Your truth set them free.

We declare every curse has been broken and Your word will heal them of everything that has plagued their souls and deliver them from the things they have experienced in this life.

Thy Word Lord we send to heal their hearts and renew their minds, and we release Your power that will give them what they need to overcome every weakness and every doubt.

The Blood of Jesus covers them, and they are blessed.

Let's take one minute to pray in the Spirit to seal this prayer for our kids. Then we say "Amen," in agreement that it is done.

> *No evil befalls my children, nor does any plague or calamity come near them. Psalm 91:10*

> *For all the promises of God in Him are Yes, and in Him Amen, to the glory of God through us. 2Corinthians 1:20*

> *Though I walk in the midst of trouble, You will revive me; You will stretch out Your hand Against the wrath of my enemies, And Your right hand will save me. The LORD perfects everything that concerns my child. Your mercy, O LORD, endures forever; You do not forsake the works of Your hands. Psalm 138:7-8*

> *The entrance of Your words gives light; It gives understanding to the simple. Psalm 119:130*

God's Peace Upon Our Children – Prayer 6

Today we pray for peace to our children, grandkids, and this next generation. In this world filled with people in great anxiety we pray that they will hear the voice of the Spirit speaking to them and calling them into their destiny.

We pray that faith, hope and love surround them. We speak God's mercy over them and His grace to empower them with strength. We release the love of God upon their generations by the Holy Ghost.

By the power of the Holy Spirit, we speak Your kingdom of righteousness, peace, and joy in the Holy Ghost over their lives. You Lord, are our peace that passes all understanding, and we cover our children with Your heavenly peace.

Let's pray in the Spirit for one minute to seal this prayer for our kids. We come in agreement by saying, "Amen".

> *Now when He was asked by the Pharisees when the kingdom of God would come, He answered them and said, "The kingdom of God does not come with observation; nor will they say, 'See here!' or 'See there!' For indeed, the kingdom of God is within*

you." Luke 17:20-21

...For the kingdom of God is not eating and drinking, but righteousness and peace and joy in the Holy Spirit. Romans 14:17

Flee also youthful lusts; but pursue righteousness, faith, love, peace with those who call on the Lord out of a pure heart. 2Timothy 2:22

Now the fruit of righteousness is sown in peace by those who make peace. James 3:18

Be anxious for nothing, but in everything by prayer and supplication, with thanksgiving, let your requests be made known to God; and the peace of God, which surpasses all understanding, will guard your hearts and minds through Christ Jesus. Philippians 4:6-7

Faith Declarations - Prayer 7

We bless our kids and grandkids and the generations to follow. We bless them and release the Light of God to them.

Father, we speak faith, hope and love to them by Your Spirit and by others that you will use to bless our kids. Our kids are free, and we release the power of Your Kingdom unto them.

Thank You for mercy and grace upon them now. Thank You for healing their minds from every wrong thought of anxiety or confusion and immoral spirit.

We pray they have no mental, emotional, and physical disorders. We call our kids whole and healthy in spirit, soul, and body. For those that are married we call their homes blessed.

We release to those who have families that You send the Spirit of Grace to their homes and that their marriages would have peace and unity.

We declare that our children are free from fears, doubts, and unbelief and that they will walk in wholeness in spirit, soul, and body.

Let's pray in the Spirit for one minute to seal this prayer for our kids. We come in agreement by saying, "Amen".

> *For God has not given us a spirit of fear, but of power and of love and of a sound mind. 2Timothy 1:7*

> *Beloved, I pray that you may prosper in all things and be in health, just as your soul prospers. 3John 2*

Covenant Of Blessings - Prayer 8

As the original version of these prayers were released on social media, by Day 8 of praying for our kids, grandkids, and the next generation, we began to receive testimonies of God touching our kids. Hallelujah. Amen.

My God is a good God. He says suffer the children and forbid them not for such are the Kingdom of Heaven. God loves our kids and hasn't forgotten His promises.

So, I call our kids blessed surrounded in faith, hope and love. I speak grace and mercy unto them. I declare they have a sound mind. They are covered in the Blood of Jesus.

We send ministering angels unto them. We speak peace and we rebuke fear, anxiety and worry off of them and release joy and confidence into their lives.

They are healed and whole in spirit, soul, and body. I speak blessings to you and your families. You are loved, Moms and Dads. Everything is going to be alright.

Now let's take one minute to pray in the Spirit to seal this prayer for our kids. Then we say "Amen," in agreement that it is done.

> *"God is not a man, that He should lie, Nor a son of man, that He should repent. Has He said, and will He not do? Or has He spoken, and will He not make it good? Numbers 23:19*
>
> *Be strong and of good courage, do not fear nor be afraid of them; for the LORD your God, He is the One who goes with you. He will not leave you nor forsake you. Deuteronomy 31:6*
>
> *Oh, give thanks to the LORD, for He is good! For His mercy endures forever. 1Chronicles 16:34*
>
> *Praise the LORD! Oh, give thanks to the LORD, for He is good! For His mercy endures forever. Psalm 106:1 (also Psalm 107:1, Psalm 118:1, Psalm 118:29, and Psalm 136:1)*

Family Intercession - Prayer 9

Today I pray for parents and their children, that God will heal and restore relationships. I speak forgiveness and for love to grow. Father, I pray that You will strengthen the parents and give them rest from fear and worry.

Remove their hurt and give them peace. We call our kids blessed. They are covered in the Blood of Jesus. Cover them as the apple of Your eye. I pray that the mercy and grace of God are upon them every moment of the day. They are strong and whole, spirit, soul, and body. Fill their hearts and minds with Your spiritual wisdom, knowledge and understanding.

I call the right people into the lives of our children. Heal their hearts from all the wounds of the past. We call them into their God given purpose in Jesus' Name. We declare that ur kids are blessed, and release ministering angels to them now.

Let's take one minute to pray in the Spirit to seal this prayer for our kids. Then we say "Amen," in agreement that it is done.

Now I say that Jesus Christ has become a servant to the circumcision for the truth of God, to confirm the promises made to the fathers. Romans 15:8

And you, fathers, do not provoke your children to wrath, but bring them up in the training and admonition of the Lord. Ephesians 6:4

Wives, submit to your own husbands, as is fitting in the Lord. Husbands, love your wives and do not be bitter toward them. Children, obey your parents in all things, for this is well pleasing to the Lord. Fathers, do not provoke your children, lest they become discouraged. Colossians 3:18-21

Now may the God of peace Himself sanctify you completely; and may your whole spirit, soul, and body be preserved blameless at the coming of our Lord Jesus Christ. 1Thessalonians 5:23

Now may the God of peace who brought up our Lord Jesus from the dead, that great Shepherd of the sheep, through the Blood of the everlasting covenant, make you complete in every good work to do His will, working in you what is well pleasing in His sight, through Jesus Christ, to whom be glory forever and ever. Amen. Hebrews 13:20-21

Release Of Divine Generational Destiny – Prayer 10

We call our sons and daughters blessed and free from any attack that would try to bring destruction to their lives.

We call them into their God given destiny, speaking faith, hope and love over them. We declare God's grace and mercy over them and into their futures. We call them restored and reformed to God's original plan for their lives.

Me and my household or family shall be saved. We release ministry angel over them, and no weapon formed against them will prosper.

We release the anointing of God over them, and we smear and apply the anointing oil, consecrating them unto the Lord – removing every burden and destroying every yoke. Let the Christ anointing cover them and deliver them from every bondage or stronghold. I call them anointed for the Master's use. Be blessed.

Now let's take one minute to pray in the Spirit to seal this prayer for our kids. Then we say "Amen," in agreement that it is done.

Prayer Of Protection - Prayer 11

Today we pray for the generations of boys and girls, men, and women—including our own kids and grandkids—that have been or are being abused physically, mentally, or emotionally. We stop it now! In Jesus' Name we cut off all those bringing abuse them from their lives.

Lord, deliver them and protect them from their abusers. That includes those babies still in the womb. We speak for the abuse in all forms physical, mental, and emotional to stop NOW! We speak faith, hope, and love and a sound mind unto these kids of all ages.

We ask You, Holy Spirit to move upon and on behalf of our kids in these situations. Remove them from every abusive relationship and household. We bring them to our Heavenly Father's care and protection.

We cover them with mercy and grace. We declare by the Blood of Jesus that they are free from every abuse, bondage, and deception. We call them healed from every form of abuse they may have experienced, and we speak divine health over them. We speak great joy and peace to them in Jesus' Name.

Now let's take one minute to pray in the Spirit to seal this prayer for our kids. Then we say "Amen," in agreement that it is done.

He who dwells in the secret place of the Most High Shall abide under the shadow of the Almighty. I will say of the LORD, "He is my refuge and my fortress; My God, in Him I will trust." Surely He shall deliver you from the snare of the fowler And from the perilous pestilence. He shall cover you with His feathers, And under His wings you shall take refuge; His truth shall be your shield and buckler. You shall not be afraid of the terror by night, Nor of the arrow that flies by day, Nor of the pestilence that walks in darkness, Nor of the destruction that lays waste at noonday.

A thousand may fall at your side, And ten thousand at your right hand; But it shall not come near you. Only with your eyes shall you look, And see the reward of the wicked. Because you have made the LORD, who is my refuge, Even the Most High, your dwelling place, No evil shall befall you, Nor shall any plague come near your dwelling; For He shall give His angels charge over you, To keep you in all your ways. In their hands they shall bear you up, Lest you dash your foot against a stone. You shall tread upon the lion and the cobra, The young lion and the serpent you shall trample underfoot. "Because he has set his love upon Me, therefore I will deliver him; I will set him on high, because he has known My Name. He shall call upon Me, and I will answer him; I will be with him in trouble; I will deliver him and honor him. With long life I will satisfy him, And show him My salvation." Psalm 91

Release Of Health And Wholeness - Prayer 12

I pray this morning concerning all situations that are causing stress upon the children and the parents of this and the next generation. I pray for God's intervention of grace and mercy.

I pray wholeness to them in their spirit, soul, and body, and rebuke sickness, diseases, and mental anxiety or illnesses in the Name of Jesus.

I release the healing power of God. I call upon Your righteousness, Holy Father. Let righteousness rule and reign in our families. Your righteousness brings everything to order with heaven, and God's image and likeness. I rebuke witchcraft of drugs and immorality off their lives, and I speak peace and favor and love to overtake our sons and daughters and our homes.

We pray for backsliding parents who have become deceived. Set them free, Holy Spirit. Remove the pride, the foolishness, and selfishness from the parents so that they would set the example of a God-fearing life.

We call our kids healed and blessed. No weapon formed against them shall prosper. We cover them with faith, hope and love. We bless our children.

Now let's take one minute to pray in the Spirit to seal this prayer for our kids and families. Then we say "Amen," in agreement that it is done.

> *No weapon formed against you shall prosper, And every tongue which rises against you in judgment You shall condemn. This is the heritage of the servants of the LORD, And their righteousness is from Me," Says the LORD. Isaiah 54:17*
>
> *I speak in human terms because of the weakness of your flesh. For just as you presented your members as slaves of uncleanness, and of lawlessness leading to more lawlessness,*

so now present your members as slaves of righteousness for holiness. Romans 6:19

For He made Him who knew no sin to be sin for us, that we might become the righteousness of God in Him. 2Corinthians 5:21

…Who Himself bore our sins in His own body on the tree, that we, having died to sins, might live for righteousness—by whose stripes you were healed. 1Peter 2:24

THE KINGDOM OF GOD

Our children deserve a better world and a wonderful life.

Only the culture of the Kingdom of God will give them (and us) that better world, because only the true Ekklesia/church can legislate God's order in the earth.

For God so loved the world that He gave us His son that none will perish but have everlasting life. Only His love can bring down the systems of this world which are immoral, rooted in hate, and in need for power. Systems that promote hatred, division, and violence. Systems that are anti-children with agendas of abortion, filth-filled education, wrong identity, and confusion.

These systems are filling our cities with homelessness, drugs, perversion, poverty, and murder. It is these leaders of unrighteousness that have set the culture in our communities – cultures of destruction.

But God hears the cries of His leaders and the parents and grandparents of His kingdom. It's only the cries of a church people that can break the influence of darkness. It's only the church that can give the children and families a place to learn the culture of heaven in earth.

That's why the enemy has influenced many believers to stay out of church, so that only the world's systems can influence them and their children. The house of God is where parents need to take their children – where they can be a part of the army of Light, bringing the whole world back into its designed purpose as when God created it.

God's' holy assembly must not be forsaken. It is the only hope that we have to change the world that our children will have to live in.

The Lord's Church shall rise again to represent the truth, having a culture that identifies with the likeness and image of our Creator.

The Body of Christ and its corporate oneness will change this world as we assemble with one another. Let's do our part to give our children a better world. Let's get back to the house of God.

Words Of Deliverance – Prayer 13

Today I pray, *"Thy Kingdom come, Lord. Thy will be done in our children."* I pray hope, faith, and love over them. I rebuke depression and hopelessness and speak strength to overcome every temptation.

We bless our children and declare the comfort of the Holy Ghost upon them.

I speak healing and deliverance from every curse, bondage, and deception. I call our kids blessed and with great favor.

We speak with the power and authority that is given to us by Christ, and as we speak over our children, every ungodly force is broken from influencing or deceiving them. They are free in Jesus' Name, and he who the Son sets free is free indeed.

Now let's take one minute to pray in the Spirit to seal this prayer for our kids. Then we say "Amen," in agreement that it is done.

> For the law of the Spirit of life in Christ Jesus has made me free from the law of sin and death. 3For what the law could not do in that it was weak through the flesh, God did by sending His own Son in the likeness of sinful flesh, on account of sin: He condemned sin in the flesh, that the righteous requirement of the law might be fulfilled in us who do not walk according to the flesh but according to the Spirit. Romans 8:2-4
>
> Therefore if the Son makes you free, you shall be free indeed. John 8:36

Releasing The Blood Of Jesus – Prayer 14

I speak wisdom and spiritual understanding over our sons and daughters. Father, we ask that You give our kids a heart of kindness, gentleness, and generosity.

We lift them up out of any pit of the enemy. We call them covered with faith, hope and love. We speak grace and mercy that will cover them and empower them. Fill them with joy and health Lord and bless them with fruitful lives.

We speak the power of the Blood of Jesus that gives life and protects them from all evil. Lord, we know that by Your Blood, our children will be cleansed and made whole with Your DNA, living their lives as sons of God.

We thank You for our kids, Lord and we bless them and call them into their purpose. By the Blood of Jesus, we have access to the Throne of Grace, to the Holy of holies and we receive Your mercy over our lives and families by the ark of Your covenant.

Now let's take one minute to pray in the Spirit to seal this prayer for our kids. Then we say "Amen," in agreement that it is done.

> Behold, I give you the authority to trample on serpents and scorpions, and over all the power of the enemy, and nothing shall by any means hurt you. Luke 10:19

> Now may the God of peace who brought up our Lord Jesus from the dead, that great Shepherd of the sheep, through the blood of the everlasting covenant, make you complete in every good work to do His will, working in you what is well pleasing in His sight, through Jesus Christ, to whom be glory forever and ever. Amen. Hebrews 13:20-21

> Let us therefore come boldly to the throne of grace, that we may obtain mercy and find grace to help in time of need. Hebrews 4:16

> But if we walk in the light as He is in the light, we have fellowship with one another, and the blood of Jesus Christ His Son cleanses us from all sin. 1John 1:7

Prophetic Release From The Seated Place - Prayer 15

We pray one minute or more for our kids, decreeing from our seated heavenly position in Christ. Father, we thank You that our kids are appointed and destined for greatness. Your mercy and grace follow and cover them. They are free from any darkness that will try to bring destruction to their lives.

Our children are covered in faith, hope and love. They are surrounded with Godly people to lift their souls. Their souls belong to you God and no evil of influence can control them. They are healed spirit, soul, and body. I speak peace and joy to their hearts.

They have self-control and I speak truth to them to set them free from every lie. They are redeemed and protected by the Blood of Jesus. No weapon formed against them shall prosper. They are God's children of righteousness, and we call then his chosen people. Amen be blessed.

Now let's take one minute to pray in the Spirit to seal this prayer for our kids. Then we say "Amen," in agreement that it is done.

> *The LORD is my shepherd; I shall not want. He makes me to lie down in green pastures; He leads me beside the still waters. He restores my soul; He leads me in the paths of righteousness For His name's sake. Yea, though I walk through the valley of the shadow of death, I will fear no evil; For You are with me; Your rod and Your staff, they comfort me. You prepare a table before me in the presence of my enemies; You anoint my head with oil; My cup runs over. Surely goodness and mercy shall follow me All the days of my life; And I will dwell in the house of the LORD Forever. Psalm 23:1-6*

> *No weapon formed against you shall prosper, And every tongue*

> which rises against you in judgment You shall condemn. This is the heritage of the servants of the LORD, And their righteousness is from Me," Says the LORD. Isaiah 54:17

Then Jesus said to those Jews who believed Him, "If you abide in My word, you are My disciples indeed. And you shall know the truth, and the truth shall make you free." They answered Him, "We are Abraham's descendants, and have never been in bondage to anyone. How can You say, 'You will be made free'?" Jesus answered them, "Most assuredly, I say to you, whoever commits sin is a slave of sin. And a slave does not abide in the house forever, but a son abides forever. Therefore if the Son makes you free, you shall be free indeed. John 8:31-36

Blessing Of Obedience - Prayer 16

The greatest blessing, we can be to our kids is by living as examples. You can't tell them how much you love God then live in sin and talk about everyone. Let's pray that the Lord heals our kids from all the bad examples they have seen in our homes and churches.

Father, we ask that You give our kids a forgiving heart of Your mercy. Help them to get free from every offence against their parents or the church. Let not their hearts be hardened because of the failures of those they trusted and looked up too.

We speak faith hope and love. We protect our kids with mercy, grace, and the Blood of Jesus – calling them forth into their God-given purposes. Help us parents to live as true followers of Christ. Bless our families Lord and restore them to wholeness and unity. We ask that You remove all divisions in Jesus' Name.

Now let's take one minute to pray in the Spirit to seal this prayer for our kids. Then we say "Amen," in agreement that it is done.

> They shall be My people, and I will be their God; then I will give them one heart and one way, that they may fear Me forever, for

the good of them and their children after them. And I will make an everlasting covenant with them, that I will not turn away from doing them good; but I will put My fear in their hearts so that they will not depart from Me. Yes, I will rejoice over them to do them good, and I will assuredly plant them in this land, with all My heart and with all My soul.' Jeremiah 32:38-41

And he will turn The hearts of the fathers to the children, And the hearts of the children to their fathers, Lest I come and strike the earth with a curse. Malachi 4:6

"…He will also go before Him in the spirit and power of Elijah, 'TO TURN THE HEARTS OF THE FATHERS TO THE CHILDREN,' and the disobedient to the wisdom of the just, to make ready a people prepared for the Lord." Luke 1:17

Thanksgiving – Prayer 17

By the 17th day of praying for our kids, God gave me this testimony: *"I have been seeing that our prayers our working. God is healing and restoring. Even with my kids' great changes have been taking place."*

Today, we speak faith, hope, and love over our kids.

We ask You Father to cover them in Your mercy and grace. Fill them with Your power and give them self-control over their flesh.

We call them blessed and may the glory of God move upon their life. We speak to their gifts to arise to bless this world with God's love in Jesus' Name. We give thanksgiving for all that you have done Lord to show Your mercy and grace unto our kids that may even be rebellious and stubborn in heart. We give you praise Lord for Your love and protecting our families according to Your promises that are given because of Christ righteousness not our own.

Now let's take one minute to pray in the Spirit and give praise to the Lord our God as we seal this prayer for our kids. Then we say (or even shout) "Amen," in agreement that it is done.

> Make a joyful shout to the LORD, all you lands! Serve the LORD with gladness; Come before His presence with singing. Know that the LORD, He is God; It is He who has made us, and not we ourselves; We are His people and the sheep of His pasture. Enter into His gates with thanksgiving, And into His courts with praise. Be thankful to Him, and bless His name. For the LORD is good; His mercy is everlasting, And His truth endures to all generations. Psalm 100

> Oh, give thanks to the LORD, for He is good! For His mercy endures forever. Psalm 106:1

> Behold, I will bring it health and healing; I will heal them and reveal to them the abundance of peace and truth. And I will cause the captives of Judah and the captives of Israel to return, and will rebuild those places as at the first. I will cleanse them from all their iniquity by which they have sinned against Me, and I will pardon all their iniquities by which they have sinned and by which they have transgressed against Me. Then it shall be to Me a name of joy, a praise, and an honor before all nations of the earth, who shall hear all the good that I do to them; they shall fear and tremble for all the goodness and all the prosperity that I provide for it.' "Thus says the LORD: 'Again there shall be heard in this place—of which you say, "It is desolate, without man and without beast"—in the cities of Judah, in the streets of Jerusalem that are desolate, without man and without inhabitant and without beast, the voice of joy and the voice of gladness, the voice of the bridegroom and the voice of the bride, the voice of those who will say: "Praise the LORD of hosts, For the LORD is good, For His mercy endures forever"—and of those

who will bring the sacrifice of praise into the house of the LORD. For I will cause the captives of the land to return as at the first,' says the LORD. Jeremiah 33:6-11

Prayer Of Integrity And Honor – Prayer 18

Father, we come to You and speak for righteousness to become the desire of our kids.

We speak integrity and honor over them. We pray into them faith, hope, and love. We cover them with Your mercy and grace. We speak the Blood of Jesus on them protecting them from every evil messenger of the enemy.

We call them blessed with peace, joy, and power to overcome weaknesses. We speak self-control and a submitted heart. Our children belong to you Lord and no weapon formed against them shall prosper. Thank You, Lord, for Your love and grace over them in Jesus' mighty Name. we call them into the will of Your kingdom and let Your glory shine upon them every day of their lives.

Now let's take one minute to pray in the Spirit to seal this prayer for our kids. Then we say "Amen," in agreement that it is done.

Canceling Demonic Assignments - Prayer 19

This prayer is for our kids and grandkids at all ages. Lord, we lift up our children to You and speak Your grace and mercy over their lives. We pray that Your will and promises be fulfilled in their lives. We speak wholeness to them in spirit, soul, and body.

They do not have a spirit of fear. They have Your Spirit of power, love, and a sound mind. We speak godliness, self-control, and wise decisions on their lives. Holy Spirit fill them and let Your anointing destroy every yoke of bondage.

I release them from anger, offences, and deception. I break every ungodly influence of friends, music, or any other wrong influence.

I say every curse, witchcraft, or words spoken against them is broken in Jesus' Name. I plead the Blood of Jesus over them. I put a hedge of protection around them. For those married or involved in a relationship, I speak peace and godly love and faithfulness to the relationship.

Thank You, Lord for blessing our kids, parents, and grandparents.

It's time to take one minute to pray in the Spirit to seal this prayer for our families. Then we say "Amen," in agreement that it is done.

> *It shall come to pass in that day that his burden will be taken away from your shoulder, And his yoke from your neck, And the yoke will be destroyed because of the anointing oil. Isaiah 10:27*

> *So I sought for a man among them who would make a wall, and stand in the gap before Me on behalf of the land, that I should not destroy it; but I found no one. Ezekiel 22:30*

> *Therefore I remind you to stir up the gift of God which is in you through the laying on of my hands. For God has not given us a spirit of fear, but of power and of love and of a sound mind. 2 Timothy 1:6-7*

Call To Fulfilled Destiny - Prayer 20

We speak faith, hope, and love unto our children. We cover them with Your mercy, grace, and lovingkindness.

We call them whole spirit, soul, and body. We speak freedom from religion and this world. Thy Kingdom come and Thy will be done in their lives. We speak the power and self-control over their flesh and wicked temptations.

We break the deception of temptation to draw them away from Your perfect will, Lord. We know that before they were born You had plans for them to do great things in the earth. Lord, they are Your sons and daughter given that they may bring others to know

You, Lord. We call them hungry for the things of God and we call their spiritual eyes to be opened to You and Your kingdom.

They are blessed and will fulfill their purposes and destiny.

Now let's take one minute to pray in the Spirit to seal this prayer for our kids. Then we say "Amen," in agreement that it is done.

> *For I know the thoughts that I think toward you, says the LORD, thoughts of peace and not of evil, to give you a future and a hope. Jeremiah 29:11*
>
> *No temptation has overtaken you except such as is common to man; but God is faithful, who will not allow you to be tempted beyond what you are able, but with the temptation will also make the way of escape, that you may be able to bear it. 1 Corinthians 10:13*

Release Of Peace And Freedom From Word Curses - Prayer 21

Today I declare God's peace over our children by removing every wrong word against them that has brought offence and hurt in their lives. Father, bring words of encouragement to them that will give them peace. We speak faith, hope, and love over our children's. We call them whole in spirit, soul, and body.

We call them blessed coming in and blessed coming out. We declare the Blood of Jesus delivering them from every word spoken against them. We call the will and purposes of God to be fulfilled in their lives. We call them into the light and for darkness to flee.

We break every word and assignment of destruction or witchcraft spoken be removed and powerless in Jesus' Name. We thank You for our children and we call them holy, fearless, and without anxiety or fear. God, we call our families blessed all the days of our lives.

Now let's take one minute to pray in the Spirit to seal this prayer for our kids. Then we say "Amen," in agreement that it is done.

> And all these blessings shall come upon you and overtake you, because you obey the voice of the LORD your God: "Blessed shall you be in the city, and blessed shall you be in the country. "Blessed shall be the fruit of your body, the produce of your ground and the increase of your herds, the increase of your cattle and the offspring of your flocks. "Blessed shall be your basket and your kneading bowl. "Blessed shall you be when you come in, and blessed shall you be when you go out. "The LORD will cause your enemies who rise against you to be defeated before your face; they shall come out against you one way and flee before you seven ways. "The LORD will command the blessing on you in your storehouses and in all to which you set your hand, and He will bless you in the land which the LORD your God is giving you. "The LORD will establish you as a holy people to Himself, just as He has sworn to you, if you keep the commandments of the LORD your God and walk in His ways. Deuteronomy 28:2-9
>
> The entrance of Your words gives light; it gives understanding to the simple. Psalm 119:130
>
> No weapon formed against you shall prosper. Isaiah 54:17

Release Creativity And Influence – Prayer 22

Because our children are the apple of Your eye, they will bring forth Your plans into this world and make this world a better place. We call our children covered in faith, hope, and love. We know that they are whole spirit, soul, and body.

They are immersed in wisdom and creativity as leaders in this world. We speak boldness and confidence unto them and great abilities beyond the abilities of those in this world. Our children are free from fear of man to accelerate into high-ranking positions in this world. They will be the influencers of this world bringing others into the kingdom of our God.

They are blessed with favor and peace. We thank you Lord for helping us bless our children as kings and priest in Your kingdom.

Now let's take one minute to pray in the Spirit to seal this prayer for our kids. Then we say "Amen," in agreement that it is done.

> All your children shall be taught by the LORD, And great shall be the peace of your children. Isaiah 54:13

> For thus says the LORD of hosts: "He sent Me after glory, to the nations which plunder you; for he who touches you touches the apple of His eye. Zechariah 2:8

Call For Prodigals To Return - Prayer 23

Today I declare our households shall be saved. Our children our given to us by the Lord and His hand is upon them. Our children our covered with mercy, they are protected while they are in their foolishness and rebellion.

They are covered with the Blood of Jesus and protected by the Blood from every evil Spirit of death and lawlessness. Our children will never be addicted to drugs or rebels against the laws of the land, and they will never live a life of incarceration. They are children of honor and respect.

They are whole spirit, soul and body and no weapon formed against them shall prosper. They are blessed and the Kingdom of righteousness will deliver them from all unrighteousness.

Now let's take one minute to pray in the Spirit to seal this prayer for

our kids. Then we say "Amen," in agreement that it is done.

> So they said, "Believe on the Lord Jesus Christ, and you will be saved, you and your household." Acts 16:31

> The Parable of the Prodigal Son - Luke 15:11-24

Declaration Of Light – Prayer 24

Lord, we thank You for our kids. We ask You to let Your light shine in their lives. We say to our kids, "Arise, and shine for the Light has come, and the glory of the Lord rises upon you."

Father, bless them with Your kindness and free them from every form of darkness. Let Your Light expose all that is not of You Lord, they are the sons of Light. Fill them with Your faith, hope, and love. Let Your light shine brighter every day in their lives.

Remove every mental, emotional, or physical sickness and let the Light of Your word bring them into Your promises. Give them self-control from ungodly desires that come hidden within the deceiving angel of light. Let Your divine plan for their lives be fulfilled as they walk as children of the Light.

Now let's take one minute to pray in the Spirit to seal this prayer for our kids. Then we say "Amen," in agreement that it is done.

> But the path of the just is like the shining sun, That shines ever brighter unto the perfect day. Proverbs 4:18

> "You are the light of the world. A city that is set on a hill cannot be hidden. Matthew 5:14

> For you were once darkness, but now you are light in the Lord. Walk as children of light. Ephesians 5:8

But all things that are exposed are made manifest by the light, for whatever makes manifest is light. Ephesians 5:13

A WORD TO PARENTS

Parents, when you have small kids still in the house, take that time while they are still home to put as much of God in them as you can.

They will only be as close to God as you are.

When you don't talk God, live God, and serve God all the way, neither will Your kids.

Don't wait until they are older, and they love the world more then they love God.

Start now and be the example to Your children.

Bring God in Your house by making the Word, worship, and prayer part of your family.

This is more important than taking them shopping and watching ungodly movies. God gave you those children and it's your responsibility to show them the way of the Kingdom.

Go to church as much as you can and show them how important it is to be a part of the family of God.

Jesus loves the children so much that He gave His life for them.

Now is the time for you to lay down your life for them as well by being a Godly example.

Let God's Truth Be Revealed - Prayer 25

We pray for the truth to be revealed by the Holy Spirit that sets our kids free. Holy Spirit, arrest them by Your power and let Your anointing flow to them, setting them free. Heal their broken hearts and deliver them from their captivities.

We pray for divine intervention and movement of Christ in their lives. We speak mercy and grace over them. Holy Spirit be their Helper to overcome weaknesses and wrong desires. Bring them to wholeness spirit, soul, and body.

We call our children blessed and at peace from every worry or anxiety. Let Your goodness bring their hearts to repentance, change, and transformation.

We call forth ministering angels over them—keeping them from everything that's destructive or evil. They are kings and priests, and our inheritance as blessings of the Lord. Strengthen the parents and give them wisdom over their children. Help each parent to stay in **the Love that never fails**.

Now let's take one minute to pray in the Spirit to seal this prayer for our kids. Then we say "Amen," in agreement that it is done.

> But to which of the angels has He ever said: "SIT AT MY RIGHT HAND, TILL I MAKE YOUR ENEMIES YOUR FOOTSTOOL"? Are they not all ministering spirits sent forth to minister for those who will inherit salvation? Hebrews 1:13-14

Blessings Over The Lives Of Our Children - Prayer 26

The Word of God says that our children are a gift from the Lord and a reward. They are a blessing and are born to overcome and prosper in this life. Our children are blessed and educated for success, and they have wisdom from the Father.

They will have a good long and satisfying life and will be the head and not the tail. They will walk in humility and submit themselves unto the Lord and His grace shall be upon them.

They are covered with the prayers of the righteous and will to the will of God. We send ministering angels unto them to serve them and protect them from all those who have set traps for their lives. We declare hope faith and love in their souls. We cast down every ungodly imagination of the is world. We declare every fear and anxiety is broken from their lives. They walk in honor of authority and do things from a pure heart.

They walk in forgiveness and without offence. Thank You Lord for keeping our kids from violence and destruction. We speak a hedge from protection and great favor over them.

Now let's take one minute to pray in the Spirit to seal this prayer for our kids. Then we say "Amen," in agreement that it is done.

This Book of the Law shall not depart from your mouth, but you shall meditate in it day and night, that you may observe to do according to all that is written in it. For then you will make your way prosperous, and then you will have good success. Joshua 1:8

Behold, children are a heritage from the LORD, the fruit of the womb is a reward. Psalm 127:3

For the weapons of our warfare are not carnal but mighty in God for pulling down strongholds, casting down arguments and every high thing that exalts itself against the knowledge of God, bringing every thought into captivity to the obedience of Christ, and being ready to punish all disobedience when your obedience is fulfilled. 2 Corinthians 10:4-6

> *Confess your trespasses to one another, and pray for one another, that you may be healed. The effective, fervent prayer of a righteous man avails much. James 5:16*

Travailing For Our Children - Prayer 27

Today I cry out in travail for our children. My heart is heavy for our kids. I break all ungodly influence and deceptions. God, Your Word says You would teach our children and lead them to peace.

We speak the Blood, grace, and mercy of our God over our children. Father, we speak Your kingdom come and Your will be done in their lives.

God, have mercy on those that are lost. Save them by Your goodness bringing them to repentance. Heal their hearts and remove toxic and poisoned memories. Give them strength Holy Spirit to overcome all temptation. You lead them not into temptation, You deliver them from evil.

We call them covered in the anointing and bless them with all Your promises. Father, draw them to You and let them know Your everlasting love.

Show them Your power and let Your kindness be known by them.

Now let's take one minute to pray in the Spirit to seal this prayer for our kids. Then we say "Amen," in agreement that it is done.

> *For You are my rock and my fortress, therefore, for You name's sake, lead me and guide me. Psalm 31:3*

> *I will instruct you and teach you in the way you should go; I will guide you with My eye. Psalm 32:8*

Our Children Are Overcomers - Prayer 28

Our kids will be overcomers of this world's lust, pride of life, and lust of the eyes. They walk in Your Spirit, and they will not fulfill the lust of the flesh. They will walk by faith and not be sight, and they will trust the Lord with all their hearts. They will be equipped and brought into the unity of the faith into the full measure and stature of Christ.

They will fulfill their God-given destiny. They will live in freedom from all destructive devices. They will be drug free and live free of anxiety. I rebuke depression and oppression off of their lives.

Great is the Lord! My God will show them His power and give them all that He has promised. They will be strong in the Lord and the power of His might over every wrong desire.

Hallelujah! Now let's take one minute to pray and praise in the Spirit to seal this prayer for our kids. Then we say "Amen," in agreement that it is done.

> *For all that is in the world—the lust of the flesh, the lust of the eyes, and the pride of life—is not of the Father but is of the world. And the world is passing away, and the lust of it; but he who does the will of God abides forever. 1John 2:16-17*

> *I say then: Walk in the Spirit, and you shall not fulfill the lust of the flesh. Galatians 5:16*

> *For we walk by faith, not by sight. 2Corinthians 5:7*

> *And then our immaturity will end! And we will not be easily shaken by trouble, nor led astray by novel teachings or by the false doctrines of deceivers who teach clever lies. But instead we will remain strong and always sincere in our love as we express*

the truth. All our direction and ministries will flow from Christ and lead us deeper into him, the anointed Head of his body, the church. Ephesians 4:14-15 TPT

PART TWO

In the reverent and worshipful fear of the Lord there is strong confidence, and His children shall always have a place of refuge.

Proverbs 14:26

Thanksgiving For Our Children - Prayer 31

Lord, thank You for giving us the offspring that have been put on this earth by You. Our children are a gift from you, given to us as a blessing. All that is not a blessing from our kids is from this ungodly world. I command it to stop, and I speak faith, hope, and love to our kids, young and old.

They will be blessed and covered in Your mercy and grace.

Let every desire that is ungodly be broken from them. Give them peace and teach them by Your goodness. We cover them in Your Blood.

I declare nothing formed against our children will succeed. They will humble themselves to Your perfect will and they will overcome every evil. I speak the power of the Holy Spirit over their lives in Jesus' Name.

Holy Spirit draw them to the Father and bring them into Your Kingdom revelation.

Now let's take one minute to pray in the Spirit to seal this prayer for our kids. Then we say "Amen," in agreement that it is done.

Victorious Through Testings And Trials - Prayer 32

Dear Lord, thank You for the faith that calls for that which is not until it is. We call our children victorious. As they go through times of testing, You will bring them through. We declare our children are sober in all areas. Sober from alcohol and drugs. Sober-minded and free from ungodly strongholds. Thank You that the god of this age has no more power to blind or deceive our kids.

Our kids are full of Your glory as the sons of God. They are justified and sanctified by faith in You, Lord. They will reign in life by Your righteousness. We speak the royalty and the glory of heaven over their lives. Create in them a clean heart and renew a right spirit in them.

They are taught of the Lord and great is their peace.

Father You are their provider of all things. Let the love that never fails bring them into Your will Lord. We speak wisdom and maturity over their lives. In Jesus' Name

Now let's take one minute to pray in the Spirit to seal this prayer for our kids. Then we say "Amen," in agreement that it is done.

> Create in me a clean heart, O God, and renew a steadfast spirit within me. Psalm 51:10

> And all your [spiritual] children shall be disciples [taught by the Lord and obedient to His will], and great shall be the peace and undisturbed composure of your children. Isaiah 54:13 AMPC

Heart Cry For Our Children - Prayer 33

Lord, we cry out of great desire to see our kids blessed by You. We know how much You love us and will do everything to help us with our kids. Father give us the patience we need and help us to discern properly without assumptions. We trust You Father to bring our kids into Your will and the purpose that You have planned for them.

No weapon formed against them or us, Lord will prosper. We cast every parental care onto You Lord, and we know You will supply all that we need to raise our kids in the right way, with a good education and a good home. We believe that we shall be blessed as we continue to put our trust in You Lord.

Help us to be the example that we need to be before our children.

Now let's take one minute to pray in the Spirit to seal this prayer for

our kids. Then we say "Amen," in agreement that it is done.

Prayers For The Prodigals - Prayer 34

Today we pray for the prodigal sons and daughters. We will never give up on them, just as the Father never gave up on us. They may be living with the piggish things of life right now, but we declare that they shall come back to the Father's house.

We pray that God will hide them in His mercy and change them by His grace. Lord, we ask that you teach all parents how to move with Your word in winning over the souls of their children. Let the parents deal with their kids by grace, not the law of religion. We call all our kids free from the bondwomen of the flesh.

We speak sober minds and hearts, and say that Your Kingdom comes and Your will is done in their lives. We speak to their designed godly destiny to come to pass. We speak their God given gifts to come forth. We honor You Father, and we know that You will give us the desires of our heart as parents.

Now let's take one minute to pray in the Spirit to seal this prayer for our kids. Then we say "Amen," in agreement that it is done.

> So then, brethren, we are not children of the bondwoman, but of the free. Galatians 4:31

Thanksgiving For Godly Help - Prayer 35

I am thankful to God for helping us with our kids. He is our Helper that brings our kids into their purpose. We declare our kids will never be defeated or taken by the kingdoms of this world.

Our kids are blessed and hidden in His mercy and they shall not be condemned with this world. Father make our kids one with You that they may testify of Your goodness. We pray in the Spirit, bringing everything into Your perfect will. We know that all things will work together for the good to them that love You.

The Righteousness of Christ will prevail in their lives. I cast down all principalities, powers, and rulers of darkness of this world. I speak the whole armour of God over our lives; our loins girded about with truth, our feet shod with the preparation of peace, we take our breast plate of righteousness, the helmet of salvation, the shield of faith and the sword of the Spirit. We stand against all the wiles and methods of the enemy.

Now let's take one minute to pray in the Spirit to seal this prayer for our kids. Then we say "Amen," in agreement that it is done.

We are assured and know that [God being a partner in their labor] all things work together and are [fitting into a plan] for good to and for those who love God and are called according to [His] design and purpose. Romans 8:28 AMPC

Finally, my brethren, be strong in the Lord and in the power of His might. Put on the whole armor of God, that you may be able to stand against the wiles of the devil. For we do not wrestle against flesh and blood, but against principalities, against powers, against the rulers of the darkness of this age, against spiritual hosts of wickedness in the heavenly places. Therefore take up the whole armor of God, that you may be able to withstand in the evil day, and having done all, to stand. Stand therefore, having girded your waist with truth, having put on the breastplate of righteousness, and having shod your feet with the preparation of the gospel of peace; above all, taking the shield of faith with which you will be able to quench all the fiery darts of the wicked one. And take the helmet of salvation, and the sword of the Spirit, which is the word of God; praying always with all prayer and supplication in the Spirit, being watchful to this end with all perseverance and supplication for all the saints... Ephesians 6:10-18

Removal Of Generational Curses - Prayer 36

Thank You Father for blessing our kids and for Your protection from all evil. We declare every generational curse is broken off their lives, speaking from our seated position of authority in the heavenly places. We speak from a place of intercession over our kids and we will declare the will of the Lord over our kids

We tear down every spiritual wickedness abiding over our kids. Your grace is sufficient to empower them to overcome every temptation and to help them to walk in their new creation as the sons of God.

They are blessed and highly favored with great courage and power to live as overcomers. They are our heritage and under Your promises by Your covenant. Lord keep them and show them Your salvation. You oh Lord are faithful to hear the cry of Your children. Hear the cries and prayers of our children Lord let them know Your ears is attentive to their cry,

Now let's take one minute to pray in the Spirit to seal this prayer for our kids. Then we say "Amen," in agreement that it is done.

> No temptation has overtaken you except such as is common to man; but God is faithful, who will not allow you to be tempted beyond what you are able, but with the temptation will also make the way of escape, that you may be able to bear it. 1 Corinthians 10:13
>
> And He said to me, "My grace is sufficient for you, for My strength is made perfect in weakness." Therefore most gladly I will rather boast in my infirmities, that the power of Christ may rest upon me. 2 Corinthians 12:9

EXHORTATION FOR PARENTS

Praying for all the parents that are hurting and living in fear. I know the things some of you suffer when Your children have become someone you don't know. When they are lost in the darkness and influence of this world. Fearing if they will die or end up in jail or hurt someone else.

You may have fear of seeing them full of depression or anxiety and unhappy. Seeing them rejecting God and falling into deception. Wondering if they will ever change. They have brought so much pain and hurt to you. They show no love or respect and yet always want you to help them.

I want you to know you don't carry that alone.

God the Father is with you and your children. He has given us promises that our seed will be a blessing. We may not see it or hear it yet, but you must keep believing Him. Don't speak what you see. Keep saying what God's word says. He has delivered many children of those parents that never gave up hope.

Don't blame yourself. I'm sure you weren't a perfect parent, none of us were. But just like you changed and God brought you out of darkness He will do the same for your children. Keep loving them and forgiving them.Keep showing them mercy, but also stand strong in telling them the truth because the word never comes back void. I was an awful son and put my parents through hell. but God came one day and set me free, right when I was in my darkest time of rebellion.

God knows how to reach our children, especially when He has us crying out for mercy and believing and trusting Him. Don't give up. Your victory will come in Jesus' Name.

God loves those children and He knows the pain you suffer.

He is there to comfort and strengthen you. Our kids shall be transformed one day to be what God has destined them to be.

Protection – Prayer 41

The word of God says if two shall agree that whatever we ask of the Father shall be done. We call Psalm 23 over our children that they will be delivered from the enemy and protected by our Father in heaven.

Our kids are covered in His mercy and they are blessed in all that they put their hand to. We speak faith, hope and love to grow in them. We break every witchcraft off of them and every word spoken against them. Every lie and every curse spoken against them is broken in Jesus' Name. They have a sober mind and free from every ungodly appetite.

They shall fulfill their purpose in God. They are without condemnation or shame but they are bold as a lion and gentle as a dove. Their sleep shall be peaceful and their hearts shall be whole. We break the spirit of fear and anxiety off of them and say that Christ's righteousness shall reign in their lives.

Now let's take one minute to pray in the Spirit to seal this prayer for our kids. Then we say "Amen," in agreement that it is done.

> Again I say to you that if two of you agree on earth concerning anything that they ask, it will be done for them by My Father in heaven. Matthew 18:19

Adulthood – Prayer 42

Lord, we cry out for our children for a move of God upon those that have entered adulthood. God help our children to lead their own kids in the ways of the Lord. Give them wisdom and discernment as they help guide them through this world.

We lift them up and speak courage to them to make right choices in regard to their kids. We pray that their faith will fail not, and we declare Satan will not sift them like wheat as they raise their kids into sons of God. They will be sober minded and steadfast and without compromise. Thank You Lord for keeping our young adults give them more mercy and grace and they lead their children in the way they should go forward in life.

Now let's take one minute to pray in the Spirit to seal this prayer for our kids. Then we say "Amen," in agreement that it is done.

> Train up a child in the way he should go, and when he is old he will not depart from it. Proverbs 22:6

Overcoming The Things Of This World – Prayer 43

Lord, we cast every care of our kids unto You. We trust You Father to cover and empower our kids to overcome the things of this world. No weapon formed against them shall prosper and everything that rises against them shall be defeated. I call them free, for he who the Son sets free is free indeed.

We speak Your power and Your glory upon them as they walk in the righteousness You have provided for them. We break every stronghold from their minds and speak the mind of Christ over them.

We call Godly people and influences into their lives. They shall fulfill their God-given destiny. They are blessed and no temptation shall overcome them. Their hearts are pure and without offence or unforgiveness. Thank You Lord for blessing our kids."

Now let's take one minute to pray in the Spirit to seal this prayer for our kids. Then we say "Amen," in agreement that it is done.

> Therefore humble yourselves under the mighty hand of God, that He may exalt you in due time, casting all your care upon Him, for He cares for you. 1Peter 5:6-7

Our Seed Is Blessed - Prayer 44

We declare our seed shall be blessed for they are the seed of Abraham, the father of faith. We call our children to their destiny and purpose in the Lord

Jesus, I give thanks from a grateful heart for all that You do for me and my family. We worship you in Spirit and in truth knowing that Your presence will never leave us or forsake us.

We call our kids into their kingdom rule and reign as sons of God. We call them into Your anointing Lord, destroy every stronghold off their minds. We speak joy into their live the joy unspeakable that will give them strength. Every choice they make will be one of wisdom and Your wisdom will cause them to prosper. Our kids are the apple of Your eye God, and they shall abide under the shadow of the Almighty.

They are hidden in Your mercy and empowered by Your grace. They shall reign in Your righteousness and subdue the earth as those of Your kingdom. I call them delivered from the kingdoms of this world influences. Your glory Lord shall rest upon them every day of their lives.

Now let's take one minute to pray in the Spirit to seal this prayer for our kids. Then we say "Amen," in agreement that it is done.

> *It shall come to pass in that day That his burden will be taken away from your shoulder, And his yoke from your neck, And the yoke will be destroyed because of the anointing oil. Isaiah 10:27*

> *Keep me as the apple of Your eye; Hide me under the shadow of Your wings. Psalm 17:8*

> *For thus says the LORD of hosts: "He sent Me after glory, to the nations which plunder you; for he who touches you touches the apple of His eye." Zechariah 2:8*

"He who dwells in the secret place of the Most High Shall abide under the shadow of the Almighty. I will say of the LORD, "He is my refuge and my fortress; My God, in Him I will trust." Surely He shall deliver you from the snare of the fowler And from the perilous pestilence. He shall cover you with His feathers, And under His wings you shall take refuge; His truth shall be your shield and buckler. You shall not be afraid of the terror by night, Nor of the arrow that flies by day, Nor of the pestilence that walks in darkness, Nor of the destruction that lays waste at noonday. A thousand may fall at your side, And ten thousand at your right hand; But it shall not come near you. Only with your eyes shall you look, And see the reward of the wicked.

Because you have made the LORD, who is my refuge, Even the Most High, your dwelling place, No evil shall befall you, Nor shall any plague come near your dwelling; For He shall give His angels charge over you, To keep you in all your ways. In their hands they shall bear you up, Lest you dash your foot against a stone. You shall tread upon the lion and the cobra, The young lion and the serpent you shall trample underfoot. "Because he has set his love upon Me, therefore I will deliver him; I will set him on high, because he has known My name. He shall call upon Me, and I will answer him; I will be with him in trouble; I will deliver him and honor him. With long life I will satisfy him, And show him My salvation." Psalm 91

Global Intercession For Our Children - Prayer 45

Leaders all over the world are crying out to God for our sons and daughters. We call them into their God given purpose. We break the influences of deception from off them. We declare that no weapon formed against them will prosper at school or the workplace.

We break every addiction of any sort, and we free their souls.

Ungodly appetites shall be broken. God has given them His Spirit, the Holy Spirit and He shall lead them to truth.

Our children are the next Kingdom of God advancers in the earth. We declare the seed of the righteous shall transform them and align them into Your perfect will Lord.

We break every ungodly soul tie and influence off of them. We separate them from friends and influences that are not of You out of their lives. We call Godly and divine relations that are ordered by You Lord to come into their lives.

Now let's take one minute to pray in the Spirit to seal this prayer for our kids. Then we say "Amen," in agreement that it is done.

Release Of Mercy - Prayer 46

Father of heaven help our children to submit to the leaders you bring into their lives. Let them not live as orphan but as sons of God. Give them their daily bread and forgive them Father of their short comings, and show them Your mercy. Help them to forgive others including their parents for their imperfections.

Heal them spirit, soul, and body. We destroy every word spoken against them and cancel every word of negativity. Lord, let Your light shine in their lives and give them revelation of who You are. My God, remove every form of discouragement or feeling of inadequacy from them. Father, give them new confidence every day.

Our kids are covered in Your Blood, Lord and hidden in Your mercy. Give them a hunger for Your word to hear it and live it. We call them blessed and overcomers in this world. Nothing shall by any means hurt them.

I speak that Your peace and the joy of the Holy Spirit shall fill their lives. They shall prosper and be blessed in all they do. In Jesus' Name.

Now let's take one minute to pray in the Spirit to seal this prayer for our kids. Then we say "Amen," in agreement that it is done.

> In this manner, therefore, pray: Our Father in heaven, Hallowed be Your name. Your kingdom come. Your will be done On earth as it is in heaven. Give us this day our daily bread. And forgive us our debts, As we forgive our debtors. And do not lead us into temptation, But deliver us from the evil one. For Yours is the kingdom and the power and the glory forever. Amen. "For if you forgive men their trespasses, your heavenly Father will also forgive you. But if you do not forgive men their trespasses, neither will your Father forgive your trespasses. Matthew 6:9-15

> Obey those who rule over you, and be submissive, for they watch out for your souls, as those who must give account. Let them do so with joy and not with grief, for that would be unprofitable for you. Hebrews 13:17

The Heart Of Our Children - Prayer 47

Holy Spirit, we ask that You move upon our children no matter what age our kids are. Fill them with a heart for our Father in heaven. We call our kids saved and on fire for God. Our kids are the next generation of Kingdom leaders in this world.

We speak the Blood of Jesus over them. We speak angels to our kids to protect and to minister to them. Give our kids dreams of the heavens and Your goodness. Send other believers to our children to help our kids to know Your power of love.

Thank You Father for Your promises and for the seeds of righteousness that will cause them to reign in life. Help them to have a pure heart and to live in peace toward all men.

Now let's take one minute to pray in the Spirit to seal this prayer for our kids. Then we say "Amen," in agreement that it is done.

Move Of The Holy Spirit – Prayer 48

Our Father in heaven, we pray for miracles for the parents who need a miracle for their kids. If they need healing or deliverance touch, them Father with Your miracle working power. We call them blessed and free in the Name of Jesus.

We lift up every son and daughter, and ask You Holy Spirit to move upon them. Fill them with the fruit of the Spirit. Help them to walk in the gifts of the Spirit. But most of all Holy Spirit, let the love of God be poured into their hearts because Your love never fails.

We pray that their hearts and souls be turned towards You Lord. We pray for those who may be in jail. Protect them and minister to them and free them. We speak the Blood of Jesus over our children. We call our kids into their callings and purpose as you have designed for them. Bless them Lord.

Now let's take one minute to pray in the Spirit to seal this prayer for our kids. Then we say "Amen," in agreement that it is done.

> *Therefore I also, after I heard of your faith in the Lord Jesus and your love for all the saints, do not cease to give thanks for you, making mention of you in my prayers: that the God of our Lord Jesus Christ, the Father of glory, may give to you the spirit of wisdom and revelation in the knowledge of Him, the eyes of your understanding being enlightened; that you may know what is the hope of His calling, what are the riches of the glory of His inheritance in the saints, and what is the exceeding greatness of His power toward us who believe, according to the working of His mighty power which He worked in Christ when He raised Him from the dead and seated Him at His right hand in the*

heavenly places, far above all principality and power and might and dominion, and every name that is named, not only in this age but also in that which is to come. Ephesians 1:15-21

EXHORTATION

Be the intercessors for Your family. Fight for their souls and their transformation. Never give up and never believe the lies the enemy says about them or what you see.

Cover them with the Word, the Blood, and the promises of God.

God's love never fails.

Declaring The Goodness Of God - Prayer 49

All evil is from the enemy and all good is from our God. So I speak God's goodness over our children, trusting that they would see His goodness and know His love.

Father fill them with Your faith and draw them by Your Holy Spirit. Speak to our kids and break every form of rebellion from their lives.

Pull them into to Your predestined planned for their lives. Keep them by Your grace and mercy and cover them with protection. I speak Your healing power over their bodies and minds. I call them into Your righteousness and Your righteous move in the earth. Restore to them all that the enemy has stolen from them.

We declare that their hope, faith, and love grows strong in them. We remove every stronghold and appetite that is not from You, Father. Our kids are blessed now and forever.

Now let's take one minute to pray in the Spirit to seal this prayer for our kids. Then we say "Amen," in agreement that it is done.

> For I know the thoughts and plans that I have for you, says the Lord, thoughts and plans for welfare and peace and not for evil, to give you hope in your final outcome. Jeremiah 29:11 AMPC

Declarations - Prayer 50

My heart mourns in intercession for our kids of all ages. We must fight for our kids in prayer. We stand in the gap for them from our seated position in the heavens. We pray forth the will of God over our children.

We call them out of every form of darkness. We speak freedom to our children and transformation to their souls. We call them into their divine destiny. We speak wholeness to them, spirit, soul and body.

Father, let Your love flood our kids' hearts. I break every spirit of rejection and shame from their lives.

We speak spiritual wisdom, knowledge and understanding to them. We pray self-control and soundness of mind. Our children will prosper and live a good and long satisfying life.

Now let's take one minute to pray in the Spirit to seal this prayer for our kids. Then we say "Amen," in agreement that it is done.

> And may the God of peace Himself sanctify you through and through [separate you from profane things, make you pure and wholly consecrated to God]; and may your spirit and soul and body be preserved sound and complete [and found] blameless at the coming of our Lord Jesus Christ (the Messiah). Faithful is He Who is calling you [to Himself] and utterly trustworthy, and He will also do it [fulfill His call by hallowing and keeping you].
> 1 Thessalonians 5:23-24 AMPC

Release Of Kingdom Culture - Prayer 51

Let's agree that our children are blessed and shall fulfill their divine purpose. I call them free from everything that the enemy uses to plague this generation. We come against spirits trying to rob our young people from their purpose in the earth, and we shall see greater results.

Father, fill our kids with Your kingdom culture and let Your will be done in their lives. We speak courage in them to face the giants of their generation. We rebuke the demonic forces from holding our children captive to any evil work. We speak peace unto our children. We speak maturity unto them. We call them wise and strong in discernment.

They will be children of order and honor. They will never be rioters or of a rebellious spirit. They will walk in respect to others and will appreciate life. They will respect life and its blessings. We speak contentment and self-control in every area. We break every spirit of witchcraft off from their lives.

We plead the Blood of Jesus over them and call ministering angels unto them. Our seed we be a blessing unto our lives in Jesus' Name.

Now let's take one minute to pray in the Spirit to seal this prayer for our kids. Then we say "Amen," in agreement that it is done.

> And Peter answered them, Repent (change your views and purpose to accept the will of God in your inner selves instead of rejecting it) and be baptized, every one of you, in the name of Jesus Christ for the forgiveness of and release from your sins; and you shall receive the gift of the Holy Spirit. For the promise [of the Holy Spirit] is to and for you and your children, and to and for all that are far away, [even] to and for as many as the Lord our God invites and bids to come to Himself. Acts 2:38-39 AMPC

Repentance For Wrong Words Over Our Children - Prayer 52

Many times we as parents have put things on our kids. Things that keep them from wanting to serve God. Like religion, condemnation, judgement, fear, anger, our culture and a feeling of being unworthy. We have given them a false identity that has nothing to do with Christ. This has caused the next generation to run from God and run to the things of this world.

So in Jesus' Name I call out all those things we have put on our kids out of ignorance. We cast them off of our children. We speak the Blood of Jesus over their souls. Souls that have been wrongly formed. Restore them Lord if they have been taken captive by their wounds and hurts caused by us parents.

Forgive us parents and deliver our children. Forgive us for putting religion over our relationship with our children. We speak healing to the souls of our children. We call our seeds a blessing of the Lord. We don't see them as lost or rebellious. We see them through the grace and mercy of God and we see them as He sees them.

We call them anointed and blessed and with long life shall You satisfy them. Thank you, Father, for our children.

Now let's take one minute to pray in the Spirit to seal this prayer for our kids. Then we say "Amen," in agreement that it is done.

> *Fathers, do not irritate and provoke your children to anger [do not exasperate them to resentment], but rear them [tenderly] in the training and discipline and the counsel and admonition of the Lord. Ephesians 6:4 AMPC*

> *Fathers, do not provoke or irritate or fret your children [do not be hard on them or harass them], lest they become discouraged and sullen and morose and feel inferior and frustrated. [Do not break their spirit.] Colossians 3:21 AMPC*

Removal Of Shame And Condemnation - Prayer 53

We call forth the promises of God to come unto our children. We break every Spirit of condemnation and shame off of their lives.

We speak the power of the Blood over them and before them. We call every generational curse broken. We call on You, Holy Spirit to bring our kids unto the Father. Holy Spirit, only You can cause them to surrender their hearts to God. Only You, Holy Spirit can remove the hardness of hearts and melt away the walls that have been built, walls that keep them from hearing and entering into the Love of God.

Holy Spirit release Your anointing over their souls and set them free from every stronghold. We speak life and life more abundantly over them.

Now let's take one minute to pray in the Spirit to seal this prayer for our kids. Then we say "Amen," in agreement that it is done.

> THEREFORE, [there is] now no condemnation (no adjudging guilty of wrong) for those who are in Christ Jesus, who live [and] walk not after the dictates of the flesh, but after the dictates of the Spirit. [Joh_3:18] For the law of the Spirit of life [which is] in Christ Jesus [the law of our new being] has freed me from the law of sin and of death. Romans 8:1-2

Unceasing Intercession - Prayer 54

We will keep praying until the Holy Spirit moves upon all our children. Not just to get them born again, but on fire for God. Deliver them from every snare and trap of the enemy.

I expose the truth of what they are now to our kids in Jesus' Name. Help them to see Father, let Your light shine in their darkness.

Bring forth Your perfect will into their lives. Give them courage to overcome the things that seem impossible. Give them Your hope, faith, and love. We speak power, love, and a soundness of mind unto them. We command any of our kids bound by perversion or immorality to be free now.

We command every evil spirit to let them go. We speak the Blood of Jesus over our kids giving them protection, forgiveness, and life. Thank You for Your mercy, grace , and love for our children, Lord. Amen and amen. To God be the Glory.

Now let's take one minute to pray in the Spirit to seal this prayer for

our kids. Then we say "Amen," in agreement that it is done.

Declaration Of Victory - Prayer 55

Lord, we lift up every son and daughter to You. We cast every care that they are facing onto You. Every worry and fear we give to You. We call our kids whole and free from the heaviness of the systems and pressures of this world. We break off them every false spirit. We declare nothing can kill, steal, or lie to them robbing them from the abundant life.

You took everything that was against them by nailing it to the cross. The enemy's power of deception has no power over our children. Every depression or anxiety we break off them now. No weapon formed against them shall prosper.

Let them not be led into temptation but deliver them from every form of evil. We speak peace and godly dreams and thoughts unto them. They are blessed with Your glory and power. We speak ministering angels unto them. We call them free and overcomers in this life.

Now let's take one minute to pray in the Spirit to seal this prayer for our kids. Then we say "Amen," in agreement that it is done.

> He canceled out every legal violation we had on our record and the old arrest warrant that stood to indict us. He erased it all—our sins, our stained soul—He deleted it all and they cannot be retrieved! Everything we once were in Adam has been placed onto His cross and nailed permanently there as a public display of cancellation. Then Jesus made a public spectacle of all the powers and principalities of darkness, stripping away from them every weapon and all their spiritual authority and power to accuse us. And by the power of the cross, Jesus led them around as prisoners in a procession of triumph. He was not their prisoner; they were His! Colossians 2:14-15 TPT

The Will Of God Made Known - Prayer 56

Today we pray for the future Kingdom advancers in the world. We must begin to turn our hearts to our children. Starting with the prayer of intercession. We from the seated position in Christ speak God's will be done in our children. We will continue to pray knocking on the walls of unbelief, fear, rebellion, hurt, deception, abuse, immorality, religion, and every evil work.

We tear them down the works that the enemy has used to set up traps and ensnare and for our children. We speak the Blood that covers and protects our children. Our children are the future of Your glory in the earth. We speak restoration, reformation, and transformation unto our kids. We call them whole spirit, soul, and body. We bless them with faith, hope, and love flowing out of their lives.

We call their hearts whole and pure from all contamination of this world. We speak destiny of courage and success unto their families and children. Thank You, Lord, that You have sent Your Holy Spirit unto our children to draw them unto You. Let Your kingdom rule and reign in their lives, in Jesus' Name.

Now let's take one minute to pray in the Spirit to seal this prayer for our kids. Then we say "Amen," in agreement that it is done.

> *Likewise the Spirit also helps in our weaknesses. For we do not know what we should pray for as we ought, but the Spirit Himself makes intercession for us with groanings which cannot be uttered. Now He who searches the hearts knows what the mind of the Spirit is, because He makes intercession for the saints according to the will of God. Romans 8:26-27*

Words Of Honor And Thanksgiving - Prayer 57

Lord, first I thank You for our children. They are from You, and we honor them with love and kindness. We see them the way you see them through eyes of love and mercy. We speak Your abundant life unto them. We send ministering angels unto them to protect and serve their needs.

Father, we speak forth Your will in their lives. We call on You Holy Spirit to draw them and free them with Your anointing. We say our children our taught of the Lord and He will bring them forth to a victorious life in Christ. Father let Your grace be upon them in greater measures, giving them greater favor and abilities beyond their own abilities

They will overcome every hurt, nor can any destruction of any sort ever come unto them. We call our children blessed. They are overcomers, full of courage and strength.

Let's take one minute now to pray in the Spirit to seal this prayer for our kids. Then we say "Amen," in agreement that it is done.

> Yet in all these things we are more than conquerors through Him who loved us. Romans 8:37

God's Redemptive Power - Prayer 58

We call upon God's redemptive power over our children of every age. We speak faith, hope, and love unto them. Jesus, we speak the power of Your Blood over them to protect and cover them.

Father let Your likeness and image form them to represent Your Kingdom in the earth. They have Your Kingdom of righteousness, peace, and joy by the Holy Spirt within them. We call them safe and under the shadow of Your wings Lord.

We break every ungodly appetite off them. We speak the whole armor of God over them. The Armor of truth, peace, righteousness, salvation, the shield of faith and the sword of the Spirit.

Now let's take one minute to pray in the Spirit to seal this prayer for our kids. Then we say "Amen," in agreement that it is done.

Removal Of Orphan Status - Prayer 59

Lord, we lift up all those kids raised without their parents. Those raised in foster homes without their mothers and fathers. Bring them into a safe place with good people who will love them.

We also pray for these kids and speak Your mercy and grace unto them today. Bring them into their destiny Lord by Your Holy Spirit. We declare every evil work against them is broken. Every power of sexually immoral spirits is broken. We declare that every spirit of drug addiction and witchcraft (pharmakeia) is broken off of them. The power of every spirit of depression and anxiety is broken.

Every spirit of unbelief and hardness of heart broken. Every religious spirit is broken. Bring these children into Your holy love. We speak peace and joy unto them. We call these kids strong and full of courage. They shall overcome every attack and assignment sent against them in Jesus' Name. We declare these children are mighty in God and have the mind of Christ.

Now let's take one minute to pray in the Spirit to seal this prayer for our kids. Then we say "Amen," in agreement that it is done.

> *For "WHO HAS KNOWN THE MIND OF THE LORD THAT HE MAY INSTRUCT HIM?" But we have the mind of Christ. 1Corinthians 2:16*

Releasing The Miaculous - Prayer 60

We release miracle working power that brings change to the impossible. We call forth signs and wonders to place upon our children. They are the free, overcomers of their generation. Thank You, Lord, for Your divine protection and mercy over them.

Their minds are free and whole and they are being transformed into the image of Christ from glory to glory.

Now let's take one minute to pray in the Spirit to seal this prayer for our kids. Then we say "Amen," in agreement that it is done.

> But we all, with unveiled face, beholding as in a mirror the glory of the Lord, are being transformed into the same image from glory to glory, just as by the Spirit of the Lord. 2Corinthians 3:18

A MOVEMENT

A Movement is when the Holy Spirit has heard the Father's heart. He starts moving in the earth to cause things to move towards what He heard the Father say. Then He comes upon those who the Father has selected to empower for the movement. It has nothing to do with man, but it has everything to do with the Father's will for this time and season in the world.

Only the Holy Spirit can put it together. And He is the only One that can touch the hearts of people to bring us together to see the Father's heart desire come to pass— bringing heaven and earth together as one.

> *...for in Him we live and move and have our being, as also some of your own poets have said, 'For we are also His offspring.' Acts 17:28*

◆ ◆ ◆

PART THREE

But Jesus called them to Him and said, "Let the little children come to Me, and do not forbid them; for of such is the kingdom of God. Assuredly, I say to you, whoever does not receive the kingdom of God as a little child will by no means enter it."

Luke 18:16-17

Generational Blessings - Prayer 61

As we pray generational blessings over our children, we declare that all of our children will prosper in life in every area. We call them filled with spiritual wisdom, knowledge, and spiritual understanding. We break and cancel every assignment of evil against them. We speak mercy and grace over them, and Your glory to fill them.

We call their minds free from all evil and call every stronghold broken. Lord, with long life shall you satisfy them. They shall never be seduced or deceived by witchcraft, drugs, or criminal behaviors. They shall be surrounded by the Godly and the presence of God. Thank you, Lord, for blessing our children of all ages.

We call ministering angels to go before them and behind them. They shall overcome every temptation and live a life of victory.

Now let's take one minute to pray in the Spirit to seal this prayer for our kids of all generations. Then we say "Amen," in agreement that it is done.

> One generation shall praise Your works to another, And shall declare Your mighty acts. Psalm 145:4

> Are they not all ministering spirits sent forth to minister for those who will inherit salvation? Hebrews 1:15

God's Keeping Power - Prayer 62

Lord, we know that nothing shall separate our kids from the love of God. We thank You Father for Your keeping power and the endless love You show our children.

We cover them with Your Blood and free them from every stronghold. We speak Your mercy over them and declare that Your mercies be new every day. We speak sound minds unto them and break off anxiety and any torment of the mind. Thank you, Lord, for blessing our children with rest in You.

We declare every ungodly appetite, friends, or connections be broken away from our children. We ask You Holy Spirit to draw them unto the Father. Give them dreams and visions that will draw them to Your predestined purpose for their lives.

Now let's take one minute to give praise to the Father as we pray in the Spirit to seal this prayer for our kids. Then we say "Amen," in agreement that it is done.

> *For I am persuaded that neither death nor life, nor angels nor principalities nor powers, nor things present nor things to come, nor height nor depth, nor any other created thing, shall be able to separate us from the love of God which is in Christ Jesus our Lord. Romans 8:38-39*

Releasing The Wisdom Of God - Prayer 63

Father in heaven, Thy kingdom come, Thy will be done in our children. Lead them not into temptation and deliver them from all evil.

Forgive them and help them to forgive as You have forgiven us. We call them blessed and overcomers of all the things of this world. We speak courage and strength over them. We declare the hedge of Your protection around them. We speak a sound mind and a clean heart with a right Spirit upon them.

We break every kind of foolishness off of them and we speak Your wisdom upon them Lord. They are covered in Your Blood and will walk in Your salvation.

Let's take one minute to pray in the Spirit to seal this prayer for our kids. Then we say "Amen," in agreement that it is done.

Application Of Psalm 23 - Prayer 64

The Lord is the Shepherd of our children. They shall not want. They will lay down in green pastures. You Lord will lead them beside the still waters. You will restore their souls. You will lead them to the path of righteousness.

When they face difficult times, they will fear no evil because you are always with them. Your rod and staff shall comfort them in the presence of the enemy. They will have Your anointing flow like oil over their heads on down to their feet. Your goodness and Your mercy shall be with them.

They will walk in the house of the Lord all the days of their lives. Your hedge of protection surrounds them. They are a blessed generation, and all their needs will be met. They shall be healthy in spirit, soul, and body. They are overcomers, triumphant over all that tries to come against them. Your peace Lord shall lead them, and faith shall be their shield.

Now let's take one minute to worship the Lord, then pray in the Spirit to seal this prayer for our kids. Then we say "Amen," in agreement that it is done.

Hope For The Future - Prayer 65

We declare that every year is going to be a wonderful year for our children. They will be drawn by the Holy Spirit and given a hunger for the things of God. We speak Your mercy and grace over our children.

I call on the Word of God that has been planted in them from the time they were born, to begin to grow in them. Holy Spirit bring them to the remembrance of Your word.

Holy Spirit move upon the hearts of our children and breathe on them. Cause that Word in them to come alive. Cover them Father with Your mercy and grace. We plead the Blood of Jesus over them.

We speak healing to their hearts and soul. We call our children washed in the Blood of Your covenant. We bless then and surround them with a hedge of protection in Jesus' Name.

Now let's take one minute to pray in the Spirit to seal this prayer for our kids. Then we say "Amen," in agreement that it is done.

Call For Restoration - Prayer 66

Today we call upon our God of restoration to restore all that has been stolen from our kids. Restore all that has taken from their minds, times, and purpose. We call on the angels to bring all that belongs to our kids. We ask for restoration of relationships between parents and their sons and daughters. We ask You Lord, to teach forgiveness unto our kids.

Restore emotions that have been torn by disappointments and hurts. Restore their souls Lord, to a healthy place and give them peace. Restore hearts and heal relationships between our kids and their parents.

We declare that our kids are whole spirit, soul, and body. We release mercy and grace in great measures all the years of their lives. We speak miracles of divine intervention bringing our children to their destiny.

Now let's take one minute to pray in the Spirit to seal this prayer for our kids. Then we say "Amen," in agreement that it is done.

> *"So I will restore to you the years that the swarming locust has eaten, The crawling locust, The consuming locust, And the chewing locust, My great army which I sent among you. You shall eat in plenty and be satisfied, And praise the name of the*

LORD your God, Who has dealt wondrously with you; And My people shall never be put to shame." Joel 2:25-26

Hedge Of Protection - Prayer 67

Father we believe that our children will be blessed by You. We believe that Your Spirit of grace is with them. We declare that they walk in the Blood covenant of all Your promises. They are the children of promise and Your peace will cover them.

We place a hedge of protection around them. We call our children blessed in all that they put their hands to. Lord we speak Your anointing over them, breaking every stronghold and delivering them from every evil. Thank You Lord that our children are drawn to You by Your Spirit.

We break every ungodly appetite off of our children. We declare great is their faith and love. Thank you Father for Your keeping power . Nothing shall separate them from Your love.

Now let's take one minute to pray in the Spirit to seal this prayer for our kids. Then we say "Amen," in agreement that it is done.

> But they were not able to resist the intelligence and the wisdom and [the inspiration of] the Spirit with which and by Whom he spoke. Acts 6:10 AMPC

Our Children Are Overcomers - Prayer 68

Lord, our children will overcome this world. They are children of hope, faith, and love. They are a blessed generation, and they will defeat the temptations of this world. Our children are free from religion and will not live in defeat to any devices of darkness.

The Light of God shall be upon them. The power of the Holy Spirit shall lead them to truth and grace. Your mercy Lord will deliver them from every captivity and every oppression. Our kids shall hunger for righteousness and desire to live Godly lives.

We cancel every assignment against our children by the Blood of Jesus. Our kids are free and walk in soundness of mind. Your peace Lord shall be upon them giving rest to their souls.

Now let's take one minute to pray in the Spirit to seal this prayer for our kids. Then we say "Amen," in agreement that it is done.

> Do not let yourself be overcome by evil, but overcome (master) evil with good. Romans 12:21 AMPC

Help From The Holy Spirit - Prayer 69

Holy Spirit we need Your help with our kids. We release the anointing upon their heads to free them from all captivities. Release vision and dreams upon them that will draw them to their purpose that the Father has chosen for them.

Holy Spirit let discernment between good and evil lead them. Let Your gifts and fruit manifest through them. Let the kingdom of righteousness, peace, and joy flow in them and through them. Holy Spirit, lead them to truth and draw them away from all that is ungodly and give them Your power to overcome every temptation.

Holy Spirit you are their Helper. Teach them all things that come from the Father. Let Your goodness lead them to repentance if they miss the mark. Have mercy on them when they fall short of walking in total obedience to you. They are the apple of Your eye.

Now let's take one minute to pray in the Spirit to seal this prayer for our kids. Then we say "Amen," in agreement that it is done.

> And I will ask the Father, and He will give you another Comforter

(Counselor, Helper, Intercessor, Advocate, Strengthener, and Standby), that He may remain with you forever-- John 14:16 AMPC

Call To Fullness In The Kingdom - Prayer 70

There is a change coming to our children in the years to come. We speak to the seeds of the Word that have been planted in them as children to grow.

Lord, we declare Your light to shine on that seed and Your rain to water that seed. We call our kids into the fullness of Your kingdom. No evil work can derail God's purpose and plan. We speak life unto them, the life of Your word to bring them into alignment with You Lord.

No weapon formed against them will prosper. We pull them out of foolishness and immaturity. We speak Your glory upon them Lord. We release the mercy of heaven upon them. They are children who are free from every deception, hurt, abuse and confusion. We call their souls into transformation as the sons of God.

Your will be done in their life Father God. They shall prosper in spirit, soul, body and with great wealth. They shall live a good long and satisfying life. No power of this world will bring them into darkness, for they are children of the light.

Now let's take one minute to pray in the Spirit to seal this prayer for our kids. Then we say "Amen," in agreement that it is done.

Release Of Healing And Deliverance - Prayer 71

Lord we lift up our sons and daughters to You. If any are physically sick I call for healing unto them. Those who may not be sick I cover them with the Blood. I declare no virus, infirmity, or physical illness can enter their bodies. I speak miracles to those that have deformities to be whole in Jesus' Name.

I speak to mental illness or mental sickness of any sort be gone from them now. Our kids are covered in Your covenant that's been given in Your Blood. We break every curse of mental, physical, or emotional attacks and cancel them now. We deliver every son or daughter from sicknesses caused by drugs, depression, obesity, or any other ungodly lie of the enemy. Our children are covered in Your mercy and grace, and they are whole spirit, soul and body.

We come against disabilities and we break this off of our children. Our kids are blessed and free and well in Jesus' Name. They shall be wise and full of spiritual understanding. Holy Spirit draw them unto the Father of Love.

Now let's take one minute to pray in the Spirit to seal this prayer for our kids. Then we say "Amen," in agreement that it is done.

Freedom Through God's Anointing - Prayer 72

Lord we thank You for our kids. We call them forth into Your will and purpose. We declare our children are protected and free from every destructive force of darkness. They are overcomers and nothing shall by any means hurt them. We call them triumphant and blessed all the days of their lives.

I break every assault against them to tear them down or rob them of God's purpose in their lives. We take authority and we command every spirit of fear, worry, and deception to be broken. Holy Spirit, Your anointing will be upon them freeing them from influences and appetites that are not of You Lord. We speak faith, hope, and love over them.

We speak the Blood of Jesus over them and around them. Thank You Lord that goodness and mercy shall follow them all the days of their lives.

Now let's take one minute to pray in the Spirit to seal this prayer for our kids. Then we say "Amen," in agreement that it is done.

RELATIONSHIP BUILDING

Relationships are built by trust and truth. We cover one another with love and integrity.

The enemy is always trying to divide relationships. Especially relationships of authority or God designed teams. The enemy will send people to discredit the one you have a relationship with, to poison Your thoughts towards them so that you can't see them the way you first saw them.

He intends to ruin what was meant to be a blessing to you. People do this to separate you from the one they are offended with, to draw you into their offence. This is called bringing discord and this is what God says he hates. Let no one put poison in your mind towards a relationship God has designed.

At least hear the other side. You may be surprised when you hear the full story.

Dedication To The Father - Prayer 73

Father, You knew our kids before they were born. You know them better than we do and You know how to touch their hearts. Fill their hearts with Your love by the Holy Spirit. And for those who have children in bondage to the things of this world, I break those bondages now in Jesus' Name.

We call our children free from oppression, lies and every suicide thought. We break off ungodly relationships or soul ties that are not of You, Lord. We pray for Godly relationships that will speak truth to them. Give them truth and give them understanding. We cover them in mercy and grace that will lead them to You Father. Holy Spirit move upon their hearts and open their sous to the word of God.

Lord as they call upon You, Your word says they shall be saved. We speak the whole armor of God over them truth, peace, righteousness, salvation, faith and the sword of the Spirit. Draw them into Your glory, Lord. Your glory will change them in a moment. I call them into the Light. Your Light shall remove all darkness. They are Yours, Lord and Your promises shall be fulfilled in their lives.

Now let's take one minute to pray in the Spirit to seal this prayer for our kids. Then we say "Amen," in agreement that it is done.

Born To Do The Will Of God - Prayer 74

Lord we declare the Spirit of the Lord is upon our children. They shall be mighty in God and You shall give them dreams and visions. They will walk in authority over all the works of the enemy. We call down every wall of hindrance to them having a blessed life.

We speak the power of God to rise upon our children to overcome all evil. Our kids will be filled with spiritual wisdom, knowledge, and understanding. They walk by faith and not by sight for they are children of covenant, covered with the Blood of Jesus.

They will be led by the Spirit and not the flesh. Our children will do the will of God and live a life of humility. They will walk in honor and integrity. They will live in the truth and the truth shall set them free.

Now let's take one minute to pray in the Spirit to seal this prayer for our kids. Then we say "Amen," in agreement that it is done.

Declaration Of Freedom - Prayer 75

The Christ, The Anointed One shall bring our children to freedom. They shall be free from every generational curse of the past. I call forth ministering angels unto our children. I speak to the angels to guard and protect our children from every evil or destruction.

The blessings of the Lord shall be upon our children. They are children of promise and covenant. The Blood of our Lord shall give them life and protect them from every demonic spirit. Thank you, Lord, for Your mercy and grace upon our children. Your peace shall be upon them as they live in this world. They will walk by faith, hope, and love all the days of their lives.

Now let's take one minute to pray in the Spirit to seal this prayer for our kids. Then we say "Amen," in agreement that it is done.

The Way To Live In The Light - Prayer 76

As God created the heavens and the earth, so will God create in our children the way to live in the Light. We speak illumination to their minds where darkness abides. That Your light will remove every form of darkness from their souls. Our children will not be conformed to this world but transformed by the renewing of their minds.

They have minds that are sound and minds that are free from every stronghold. We tear down every lie and deception of belief that is contrary to the word of God. Our children's help comes from You Lord, and only You can transform our children into Your sons. We open their minds to the Kingdom of God.

We call for new desires of good not evil and break every ungodly desire for the things of the world. We speak the Blood of Jesus over the minds of our children. We call them healed in their mind from any damage from life. From foods, alcohol, chemicals, drugs and from every form of perversion and deception. Our children our covered in mercy and grace and their minds shall grow into the mind of Christ.

Now let's take one minute to pray in the Spirit to seal this prayer for our kids. Then we say "Amen," in agreement that it is done.

Called Into The Will Of God - Prayer 77

My heart is heavy for our kids this morning. Father, You have given us access to You through Your son. We have been given citizenship in the heavenly places. We have been given a seat of authority with Christ, being one with Him. So, from this seated place we declare that by Your grace and mercy we draw our kids unto You. We pull them out of darkness and curses of blindness.

We call them into Your will where they can fulfill what they were destined for in this world. We release the light unto them that causes them to cry out to You for Your salvation. To those already serving You we speak greater hunger and desire for the Kingdom then ever before. We call the angels to minister to them drawing them to You.

We command principalities, powers, rulers of darkness and spiritual wickedness to step back. We cancel every one of your assignments against our kids now.

We release mercy and grace upon our kids. They shall be mighty in

God. We pull down every stronghold off of their lives. Their hearts shall be cleansed and made pure for Your glory Lord.

Now let's take one minute to praise our Father as we pray in the Spirit to seal this prayer for our kids. Then we say "Amen," in agreement that it is done.

Casting The Care Of Our Children Upon Him - Prayer 78

Lord, we lift up our sons, daughters, grandsons, and granddaughters. Father, we give every care of them to You. We refuse to fear or worry over our children.

Father give our children wisdom and enlighten their eyes to see what You want them to see. We declare our children are covered in mercy and grace, and are blessed in all that they do.

We speak the Blood of our Christ and His anointing over them. Father make them one with You and give them grace to walk in Your truth. We call forth a supply of all they need spiritually, materially, and relationally. Holy Spirit draw them unto You and fill them with Your power. In Jesus' Name our children shall live a good long satisfying life.

Now let's take one minute to pray in the Spirit to seal this prayer for our kids. Then we say "Amen," in agreement that it is done.

> Therefore humble yourselves under the mighty hand of God, that He may exalt you in due time, casting all your care upon Him, for He cares for you. 1Peter 5:6-7

Releasing Psalm 91 Over Our Offspring - Prayer 79

Father, we thank You that our children and grandchildren dwell in the shelter of the Most High and that they abide under the shadow of the Almighty. My children and grandchildren say of You, Lord that You are their refuge and fortress. You are their God, in whom they trust.

Surely You deliver them from the snare of the fowler and from the noisome pestilence. You cover them with Your feathers and under Your wings shall they trust: Your Truth is their shield and buckler. They shall not be afraid for the terror by night; nor for the arrow that flies by day, nor for the pestilence that walks in darkness nor of the destruction that lays waste at noon day. A thousand shall fall at their side, ten thousand at their right hand but it shall not come near them! Only with their eyes shall they behold and see the reward of the wicked (and turn from it).

Because they have set their love upon You Lord; and have made you their refuge, even the Most High their dwelling place, no evil shall befall them, neither shall any plague come near their homes or bodies. For You have given Your angels charge over them, to keep them in all their ways….they shall bear them up in their hands lest they dash their foot against a stone.

They shall tread upon the lion and the cobra, the young lion and the serpent they shall trample underfoot. And You

Because our sons, daughters, and grandchildren set their love upon You, Father, You will deliver them, You will set them on high because they have known Your Name! And Father, You said: "They shall call upon Me and I WILL ANSWER them; I WILL be with them in trouble; I WILL deliver them and honor them. With LONG LIFE will I satisfy them and show them My Salvation!"

We thank You Father for your words concerning our children. We thank You for the Blood of Jesus protecting them, we thank You for perfecting the things that concern our children and grandchildren.

We agree with You and Your word, and say, "It is well with our children. It is well with our grandchildren. It is well with the next generation. It is well. It is well. It is well." Amen.

Now let's take one minute to pray, praise, and worship in the Spirit to seal this prayer for our kids. Then we say "Amen," in agreement that it is done.

The Power And Strength Of God - Prayer 80

Lord we present every care of our children our sons and daughters unto You. Your power is the only power that can bring change and protection to our kids. So from our seated position with You as sons of God, we release Your power and Your strength upon our kids. Giving them power over darkness and power to overcome every temptation. Power to change what they cannot change themselves.

We trust Holy Spirit's power to draw them into Your marvelous light. As the Spirit of God moved upon the face of the earth and separated darkness from light, so we pray that same move of Your Spirit Father God. Move upon our children. Fill them with spiritual wisdom, knowledge, and understanding. Let Your power be known bringing deliverance and miracles needed to change those sons and daughters in bondage.

We break every ungodly connection and influence over their lives. Protect them with Your mercy and free them with Your love. Give them a sound mind of peace. Remove fear and anxiety far from them and strengthen them to do good. Let Your love send people of love and godly influence into their lives. We call our children blessed and full of Your grace in Jesus' mighty Name.

Now let's take one minute to pray in the Spirit to seal this prayer for our kids. Then we say "Amen," in agreement that it is done.

Breaking Of Demonic Powers - Prayer 81

Father, we come to you as our Father in faith. We declare the God kind of faith upon our kids and on the parents. We defeat the spirit of unbelief and hardness of heart off of our children and parents.

Let faith arise from you Holy Spirit. We release the anointing to break every spirit of unbelief and doubt off them now in Jesus' Name. Our children are children of faith that overcome every attack of this world. Our children's eyes are upon You Lord and they trust You to be their deliverer.

Thank you, Father, for Your word to rise up in our children, giving them faith to move mountains. We declare faith to the children and the parents in Jesus' Name.

Now let's take one minute to pray in the Spirit to seal this prayer for our kids. Then we say "Amen," in agreement that it is done.

Transformation Of Minds - Prayer 82

We pray for transformation of the mind in all our kids. We break strongholds from generational mind sets of racism and ungodly cultures. We break poverty mindsets that makes them want the handouts that keep them depending on systems of poverty.

We break slothful minds that feel everything is owed to them. We cast down minds of hate and bigotry and criticism. We loose our kids from minds of idolatry and perversion. We break every mindset of religion and false understanding. We speak minds of peace and pure minds of humility upon our children.

We speak the Blood of Jesus over their minds, removing suicide and depression from their thoughts. We call the mercy of God and His grace over our children and over their minds in Jesus' Name.

Now let's take one minute to pray in the Spirit to seal this prayer for our kids. Then we say "Amen," in agreement that it is done.

Lead Them To Repentance - Prayer 83

Lord Your word says it's the goodness of God that leads one to repentance. We speak Your goodness over our children that will bring them to change. We cancel and destroy a rebellious spirit that refuses to change. We remove the blindness from their eyes that keeps them from seeing Your goodness.

We declare they shall come to repentance if they have gone astray. Lord, we believe that You Holy Spirit will draw them to this place of change. We speak for their hearts to soften and their hearing be open to that goodness of You Lord. Let Your great love flood their lives with Your grace and mercy.

We speak the Blood of Christ our Lord over them to break through those hard places separates them from You Lord. We call them into their callings and purpose where You will help them fulfill their destiny for their lives. In Jesus' Name.

Now let's take one minute to pray in the Spirit to seal this prayer for our kids. Then we say "Amen," in agreement that it is done.

Canceling The Plans Of The Enemy - Prayer 84

We thank You Father for the children You have given us. We lift them up to You in our prayers. Knowing that You love them and have given Your son for them. We cancel the enemy's plot to mislead our children into the hands of the father of lies.

We declare our children cannot be taken from Your hand. We thank You Father for blessing our kids with mercy and grace. Now Father we deliver their souls from corruption. We speak healing to their hearts and minds. They have minds that are free from every stronghold. We release wisdom unto them and call them wise.

We cancel thesSpirit of foolishness and a deformed belief mentality. We speak Your Blood over them and put a hedge of protection around them. We cancel every destructive action of the enemy that he has plotted against them.

Our children are blessed coming in and going out. They shall live in green pastures and be filled with our Father's goodness in Jesus'

Name.

Now let's take one minute to pray in the Spirit to seal this prayer for our kids. Then we say "Amen," in agreement that it is done.

PRAYER FOR THE WEARY

We pray for heavy souls to be lifted up right now in Jesus' Name. Some of you have souls that are hurting or oppressed. Your hearts hurt because of what some of your children are putting you through.

We break it off of you in Jesus' Name. We speak peace to your souls. You shall overcome. You will not be overcome by fear and discouragement.

Your children are in God's hands.

Proclaiming Victory For Our Children - Prayer 85

Lord we are Yours now and forever. You said if we set our love upon You that You will bless our children. We call our children blessed with Your favor and Your love. We cancel every word spoken against our children with negativity or evil. We call every promise of God to come forth unto our children.

We declare that every prayer from our children will come to pass. Thank You, Father, for You will do exceedingly abundantly above all that they can ask or think. Every mountain shall be removed, and every desire of righteousness shall come to pass.

Thank You, Father, for Your mercy and grace that we speak over our children. They shall not be moved, nor shall anything bring them to defeat. They are mighty and strong, and nothing shall by any means hurt them in Jesus' Name.

Now let's take one minute to pray in the Spirit to seal this prayer for our kids. Then we say "Amen," in agreement that it is done.

> Never doubt God's mighty power to work in you and accomplish all this. He will achieve infinitely more than your greatest request, your most unbelievable dream, and exceed your wildest imagination! He will outdo them all, for His miraculous power constantly energizes you. Ephesians 3:20 TPT

Ordained From The Womb - Prayer 86

Father Yyou gave us Your son so all that we were ordained to be before we were in our mother's womb would come to pass. So I speak to our children in all they were ordained for before entering this world to come to pass. We call for maturity and wisdom to rise in our children with great understanding.

We declare that they will know who they are in Christ and have a God identity and not the worlds identity. They are delivered from every false identity that is a lie from the father of lies. We speak foor the Blood line of Christ, His DNA to manifest through our children. We protect their minds and hearts with a hedge of protection.

We send ministering angels to bring them into their true identity. We call our children into their calling that's on their lives. Nothing shall be able to hinder them. We speak this now in Jesus' Name.

Now let's take one minute to pray in the Spirit to seal this prayer for our kids. Then we say "Amen," in agreement that it is done.

> Then the word of the LORD came to me, saying: "Before I formed you in the womb I knew you; Before you were born I sanctified you; I ordained you a prophet to the nations." Jeremiah 1:4-5

Our Children Belong To The Lord - Prayer 87

The battle is not ours, it's the Lord's, so we turn our kids over to You Lord. We declare that that they will come forth in Your glory. They will not be defeated by the demonic forces of our day. We plead the Blood of Jesus over their lives. We break every rebellious and tormenting spirit that may be trying to destroy them.

We speak forth a sober mind and heart unto them. We rebuke double mindedness and foolishness off of our kids. We release ministering angels over them to guard them and keep them. We pull down every spirit of witchcraft from those addicted to drugs or perversion. We call our kids free from every power of darkness and deception. You have ordained them before they entered their mother's womb to be Your sons carrying Your identity, Lord.

We call them into a safe place with Your love and goodness bringing them to repentance. They are victorious and overcomers in Jesus' Name.

Now let's take one minute to pray in the Spirit to seal this prayer for our kids. Then we say "Amen," in agreement that it is done.

The Future Of Our Children - Prayer 88

The glory of the Lord will rise upon our children. Our children are the future generation of Your Kingdom Lord. We declare our children shall overcome and destroy the works of the enemy.

I rebuke every weak and insecure spirit off of our children. I call our children mighty in God.

We see our children as the future sons of God taking the things of God to the next level. No attack of destruction shall touch our children. The Blood of Christ will give our children liberty and protection from the rulers of this age. Our children will stop the mouths of lion and will know truth over a lie.

The Spirit of the Lord is upon our children giving them the love of God. We declare every spirit of offence and insecurity is broken from their lives. Our children do not walk in fear, but in power, love, and a soundness of mind in Jesus' Name.

Now let's take one minute to pray in the Spirit to seal this prayer for our kids. Then we say "Amen," in agreement that it is done.

> But the Lord is faithful, who will establish you and guard you from the evil one. And we have confidence in the Lord concerning you, both that you do and will do the things we command you. Now may the Lord direct your hearts into the love of God and into the patience of Christ. 2Thessalonians 3:3-5

Calling Our Children Out Of The World - Prayer 89

We lift up our kids to You Lord. We speak from a place of authority and power. We command our kids to come into alignment with the word of God. We take authority over their lives and remove every form of darkness and deception. We plead the Blood of Jesus over them and break off every lie from their minds.

We call them free from weakness, discouragement, and confusion. We declare that they will walk as children of the light and they will not be conformed to this world. We bless them with every spiritual blessing. We declare every cry from their hearts to You Lord will be answered and You will be their salvation.

You are their Healer; spirit, soul, and body. We call down every manipulation off of their lives that will try to control them and mislead them. Our kids shall live in peace and joy all the days of their lives in Jesus' Name.

Now let's take one minute to pray in the Spirit to seal this prayer for our kids. Then we say "Amen," in agreement that it is done.

Healing The Hearts Of Our Children - Prayer 90

We call upon the anointing that heals the broken hearts. We call the hearts of our children to be made pure from every poison. Heal their hearts of all that has weakened them with sorrow and discouragement.

Create in them Lord a clean heart and renew a right spirit within them. We declare that they will have a heart after You Father. We soften their hearts from every hardness and rebellion. We speak the Blood of Jesus over their hearts removing every deception and wrong desire.

We speak a heart full of love and forgiveness. We call their hearts restored to wholeness and full of Your peace in Jesus' Name.

Now let's take one minute to pray in the Spirit to seal this prayer for our kids. Then we say "Amen," in agreement that it is done.

PART FOUR

*May the Lord give you increase more
and more, you and your children.*

Psalm 115:14

Mercy Upon Our Children - Prayer 91

Father, You are the Father of fathers. You know how to reach and help our kids. You are the Father of love and patience. Your mercies are new every day. Have mercy on our kids as you did with us and deliver them from foolishness.

Give our kids wisdom to defeat the foolishness of their youth. We call them filled with spiritual wisdom, knowledge and understanding. We declare that our children will be wise as serpents but gentle as doves. Give them the wisdom from above that brings them to a wealthy place. Our children will move and live by Your truth that will set this world free.

We speak the grace of our Christ over their lives and call them the blessed of the Lord. Great favor shall be upon them Lord, because of Your amazing grace. Our children are our blessing. They will be guided by Your hand in Jesus' Name. Amen.

Now let's take one minute to pray in the Spirit to seal this prayer for our kids. Then we say "Amen," in agreement that it is done.

The Awakening Of Our Children - Prayer 92

Father, we honor You and surrender our lives to You as Your children. We submit our children to You and ask You to reach them like You have reached us. Only by Your Spirit can they be drawn to You.

We release angel visitations and dreams from You that will awaken them. We call them forth to not just be saved but their eyes opened to the Kingdom. We break them free from every kingdom of this world. We speak the Blood of our Christ and His anointing over their live.

I call them faithful to the culture of Your Kingdom Lord. We loosen them from every bondage of this world.

We break the spirit of this world off of our children. The pride, lust of the flesh, and the lust of the eyes. We call our children overcomers in this world. They are blessed and faithful sons of God.

Now let's take one minute to pray in the Spirit to seal this prayer for our kids. Then we say "Amen," in agreement that it is done.

Breaking Off Controlling Powers - Prayer 93

Lord, this world is driven by pride, lustful desires, and the lust of the eyes. I break all three of these from influencing our children.

Lord, we speak against pride and arrogance. We break the spirit of stubbornness off of our children.

I release humility and a submissive heart upon our children. Pride of destruction, you have no power over our children. We cast pride down. I break that lustful spirit of strong desires. Spirit of lust you have no power over our children. We break every generational curse of perverted lust off of our kids.

The spirits of homosexuality and pornography, we destroy you in Jesus' Name. We call for your influence and control to be broken and defeated. Every imagination of lust we cast down now, and call you powerless over our children.

We break the lust of the eyes that is that go after other people's blessing and positions, we break you off now in Jesus' Name. We declare sound minds and pure hearts and eyes of holiness upon our children.

They are overcomers of pride and lust. We call down every uncontrollable urge and ungodly need to be broken by the Blood of Jesus. Our kids will be holy and of sound minds and hearts. We speak to the seed of righteousness to grow in them bringing them to their identity in Christ. We call our children whole spirit, soul, and body.

Now let's take one minute to pray in the Spirit to seal this prayer for

our kids. Then we say "Amen," in agreement that it is done.

Providing A Cover For Life - Prayer 94

Father today we cover our kids with prayer. You said the prayers of the righteous availeth much.

We cover them first with Your mercy and grace by faith.

We cover them with Your love and we know love never fails.

We cover them with the anointing that destroys every yoke of bondage.

We cover them with the Word that will transform their lives.

We cover them with the Blood that protects, cleanses and gives life.

We cover them with hope and we break off the spirit of hopelessness.

We cover them with wisdom, giving them power to choose and make right decisions.

We cover them with humility breaking every spirit of pride.

We cover them with the comfort of the Holy Ghost calming them from every anxiety.

We cover them with peace, Your peace that passeth all understanding.

We cover them with strength, giving them power to overcome every temptation and trial they face.

We cover them with blessings for life and with right relationships.

We cover them with divine health and long life.

We bless them with all covenant blessings and call them overcomers of life.

We cover their hearts with forgiveness and honor.

Thank you, Lord, for Your hand that will be set over the children of the righteous.

Now let's take one minute to pray in the Spirit to seal this prayer for our kids. Then we say "Amen," in agreement that it is done.

Healing And Deliverance Of Their Souls - Prayer 95

I pray that our children will not just know God, but live for God. I lift up their souls today. Their minds, wills, and emotions. I pray that they would come into the mind of Christ.

We break every stronghold from their minds holding them in deception, blindness, and weakness. We declare their minds to be made whole. We call their minds whole from any damages of drugs and false knowledge.

We cast down every false thought or thinking in Jesus' Name. We call for their wills to surrender to the will of God. We speak a submitted will that will honor God's word and convictions.

Father, let Your will be done in their lives from before they were born. We speak to their emotions and call them healed, controlled, and balanced. We declare that all emotions of fear, anxiety, torment loose them now.

We speak perfect peace over their emotions. I rebuke radical out-of-control emotions—you be still in Jesus' Name.

I call our children whole in spirit, soul, and body in Jesus' Name. We break every ungodly soul tie and set them free from those ties now. We declare our children shall have a transformed soul. That they come into the image and likeness of Christ in Jesus' Name.

Now let's take one minute to pray in the Spirit to seal this prayer for our kids. Then we say "Amen," in agreement that it is done.

Speaking To Their Hearts - Prayer 96

Lord, there are so many broken hearts and hardened hearts. We ask You to heal the broken hearts of our children. Hearts that have been hardened and hearts that have been polluted. Create in our children a clean heart and give them a right spirit. Father, You never judge our kids according to their deeds, but You look into their hearts.

Father lead them out of things that are filling their hearts with lies and causing their hearts to be hard. Only You Father can touch the hearts of Your children. Minister Father by Your Holy Spirit to their hearts of unbelief. We bring their hearts back to a place of belief as a little child. We break the hardness and we speak to their heart to be soften and teachable Lord.

We speak healing to their hearts from life's experiences that they have encountered. Father we ask You to have mercy on them and once again show them Your grace as You bring their hearts back to a place of submission to You. Hearts be healed. Be free and be humbled in all our children in Jesus' Name.

__Now let's take one minute to pray in the Spirit to seal this prayer for our kids. Then we say "Amen," in agreement that it is done.__

> *Then I will give them one heart, and I will put a new spirit within them, and take the stony heart out of their flesh, and give them a heart of flesh, that they may walk in My statutes and keep My judgments and do them; and they shall be My people, and I will be their God. Ezekiel 11:19-20*

THE CORPORATE BODY

I hate what the devil does in the world with the young people. He attacks them with physical and mental sickness. He attacks them with deception and lies. His darkness in this world must go.

That's why we must put down our swords towards one another and direct them at the enemy. We must come together as the corporate Body of Christ and defeat evil from nation to nation.

God, have mercy on this world once again and fill this earth with Your glory in every nation.

Save The Children - Prayer 97

Praying for our children both young and old. We speak to their spirits to be revived. We call for an awakening to our children to the seeds of truth planted in them to come forth. We cover our kids with redemption by the Blood of Christ. We declare righteousness, justification, sanctification, and reconciliation over our children. We speak to their souls to hear from the Spirit of God. We call our children free from every generational curse.

Lord, Your salvation is Your deliverance. We speak Your salvation over our children bringing them deliverance in every area of their lives. Right now we break every wrong spirit and deception over their minds. We speak liberty to our children and we set them free from every form of darkness.

We pray for those children who are free to remain free; that they would grow in wisdom and power as overcomers in this life. Lord, we also lift up the children of this world. We ask you to protect them and cover them with Your angels.

We call for divine intervention to all those in countries where kids are starving and being used as sex slaves. Send them help Lord, have mercy my God, and save the children.

Now let's take one minute to pray in the Spirit to seal this prayer for our kids. Then we say "Amen," in agreement that it is done.

Our Households Are Saved - Prayer 98

Father we stand on the Word of God over our children of every age. We declare that all of our households will be saved. Saved from sin, curses, and eternal judgement. Our kids are redeemed by the Blood of the Lamb. They are free from every sickness, poverty, mental disorder, and anxiety.

Our kids are free from fear, worry, cares and every form of a wrong spirit. Our kids will never live as criminals or live lives in defiance to authorities. Our kids are free from rebellion or having a rebel spirit. They will not be influenced by occults, new age, demonology or witchcraft.

Our kids are covered by the Blood of Jesus and the covenant of our God. Our kids are taught of the Lord and blessed with a good, long, and satisfying life.

Father we declare that our kids are covered and wrapped in mercy and grace. We release the faith planted in their hearts to grow and increase. Bless the Lord, for He is faithful to protect and bless our seeds, now and forever. Amen.

Now let's take one minute to pray in the Spirit to seal this prayer for our kids. Then we say "Amen," in agreement that it is done.

The Righteousness Of God - Prayer 99

Lord, Your word says the prayers of the righteous avail much. We know as we pray for our kids no matter the age we will see our prayers answered. It is Your righteousness Lord, that gives us a seated place in the heavenly places. As we pray from our position as sons, we know that we enforce the rule of God in the earth.

So we pray over our children that they are to align to our prayers. They are covered by Your grace and made free from every lie. Our children will not serve sin or the father of lies. They are children of righteousness. We call forth Your righteousness to align all that's out of order in our children lives spirit, soul, and body.

Righteousness is the force of truth and the light that will set our children free.

Your righteousness Lord, will cause them to reign in life and overcome every form of darkness. Lord You became sin that we might be the righteousness of God. Father make them one with Your heart and lead them to that place that is higher in You. We call them children of righteousness, surrounded by Your angels.

We draw them in by Your Spirit Father, and call them whole in Jesus' Name.

Now let's take one minute to pray in the Spirit to seal this prayer for our kids. Then we say "Amen," in agreement that it is done.

God's Delivering Power - Prayer 100

Today we are going to release God's delivering power over the lives of our kids and grandkids, young and old. Believers or not, they are going to be delivered.

We speak their deliverance from spirits, circumstances, or addicting behaviors. They are delivered from bad relationships and ungodly soul ties. Delivered from religious spirits, new age, or doctrines of devils. We speak deliverance from poverty, sicknesses, and every evil work sent to bring destruction. They are delivered from drugs, alcohol, perversion, and voices of deception.

Deliver them Lord from gossip, ungiving hearts, unfaithful ways and laziness and from every form of witchcraft, occult, cults, and satanic religions. Deliver them from false assumptions, offences, and hearts of bitterness. Open their eyes Lord to Your salvation, bringing deliverance from every false culture, racism, and strongholds from the kingdoms of this world. We release the anointing now to set the captives free. By the Name above every Name, the Name of our Christ, our Lord, be free now.

By the authority given to us as sons of God, we command our kids to be free now in Jesus' Name. Devils, take your influences off of our kids now! We break the rebellion, and dishonor towards authority off of their lives. They will not be criminals, nor bound to the criminal systems of society. We deliver our kids now from all fears, insecurities, and doubts now, in the Name of our Lord. Now we thank You Lord for setting all our kids free in Jesus' Name.

They are the sons of righteousness, and they are blessed of the Lord. They shall succeed and overcome every trial and temptation.

I remove all desires that are ungodly from them. We speak strength to them, and confidence now in the Name of our Christ. Glory to God, our kids are free and are ambassadors of the kingdom of God. They are kings and priest now in this world. No weapon formed against them shall prosper. Praise the Lord.

Now let's take one minute to pray in the Spirit to seal this prayer for our kids. Then we say "Amen," in agreement that it is done.

Wholeness In Our Children - Prayer 101

Today's prayers are released for our children, young and old. We speak wholeness to them. We declare our kids to be made whole in spirit, soul, and body.

We pray for any of our kids that are bound with infirmities in their soul or bodies—we loose them of their infirmities. We call them whole emotionally, that they would have sound minds. We call them whole spiritually with sound doctrine and accurate understanding. We call them whole in their relationships and experiences. We speak to every unhealthy relationship and we break the soul ties.

We declare sozo over them, that they would be whole and free from all that is unhealthy for their lives and future. We call them whole from hurts, wounds, and abuses they may have experienced in this life. We call them whole and bring them into alignment with truth and their true identity.

We call them whole spiritually and awaken to the kingdom of God. We remove the scales from their eyes and the deafness of their spiritual ears. Open the eyes of their heart Lord and let them see you. We call them whole spirit, soul, and body now in the Name of our Christ.

Now let's take one minute to pray in the Spirit to seal this prayer for

our kids. Then we say "Amen," in agreement that it is done.

Changed By Truth - Prayer 102

Father God, we trust You to bring our children to truth. I declare grace and truth to empower them and free them. Lord, You are Truth. We trust You to guide our children into Your truth. Let it deliver our kids from the darkness of this world. Truth that will change their hearts and transform their souls.

Let Your truth expose the false identities and let truth bring them into their true identity. We call upon truth to move on our kids and remove from every form of blindness or deception. We break through every wrong imagination with the Spirit of Truth. We thank You Lord for establishing our children in the truth.

Truth that will give them their true life and the destiny that you planned for them before the foundations of the world.

Now let's take one minute to praise God and pray in the Spirit to seal this prayer for our kids. Then we say "Amen," in agreement that it is done.

Time For Turnaround - Prayer 103

Father, this is the day that we began to see great turnaround in the lives of our kids. We call them into their destiny and we speak Resurrection life unto them. We release the outpouring of Your Spirit to breathe upon the seed planted in their lives.

We declare that the word that's has been planted will accomplish that what it was sent forth to do, and we release the angels upon their lives to bring them into their divine calls. We cover them with the Blood of our Lord and we speak the Bread of Life unto them.

We cover them with the full armour of God, and with truth, peace, righteousness, salvation, faith, and the sword of Your Spirit. Lord, we speak that the shield of faith protects their minds from all the fiery darts of the enemy.

We declare their souls to be transformed and not conformed to this world. The hand of the Lord is upon them and no weapon formed against them shall prosper. We take authority against every deception or lie, and we expose it through discernment and with grace and truth. Bless the Lord, O my soul, and may He bless our children with all His promises.

Now let's take one minute to praise the Lord, then pray in the Spirit to seal this prayer for our kids. Then we say "Amen," in agreement that it is done.

Release Of The Word Over Our Children - Prayer 104

Today we speak the Word over our children. Thy word, O Lord, will accomplish that which it was sent forth to do— to heal and deliver our children based on Your promises.

We have trusted in Your word to transform our children out of darkness into Your light. Your word says we have been given authority over all the works of the devil. So we take authority based on being sons of God.

Sons that have been restored to our origin as having Your image and likeness. We have been restored through Your Blood. We have power in the earth over all creation. So we take authority over our children's lives. We call them forth into Your liberty. We loose them from every curse and we break every deception off of them. Our children our covered in Your Blood and protected.

We release mercy and grace over them. It's Your goodness that will lead those children from rebellion to repentance. Your love never fails Lord. Your love will bring our children to their divine calls.

You have chosen them before they were in their mothers' womb to be children of light. You have given them victory over every form of darkness. We call them blessed and overcomers. They will serve the Lord with all their souls and hearts.

Now let's take one minute to pray in the Spirit to seal this prayer for our kids. Then we say "Amen," in agreement that it is done.

Godly Wisdom As They Mature - Prayer 105

Today I speak over our kids young and old, that they may mature into perfection. I rebuke the foolish spirits trying to keep our kids in immaturity. We declare the wisdom of God upon our children.

I rebuke that which keeps them from getting understanding to the truth that will set them free. Lord, fill our kids with a heart hungry for maturity. Deliver them from false ways that are childish behaviors.

We speak maturity that gives them self-control over the desires of a fleshly and ungodly appetite. Give them the maturity to know right from wrong, and to desire good over evil. Lord, help them to have strength over the foolishness of the flesh. Deliver our children from the lies that keep them bound to false identities and false beliefs. We break the spirit of pride that leads them to foolishness.

We take authority over immature behaviors led by emotions instead of principles of truth. We speak the wisdom of God and the power to live a Godly life. Give them discernment and strength to choose right relationships. We call our children into being responsible people. We declare that our children will live a life of maturity, wisdom and great understanding. They are wise and will be the sons of God and come into full perfection.

Now let's take one minute to pray in the Spirit to seal this prayer for our kids. Then we say "Amen," in agreement that it is done.

> Wisdom and knowledge will be the stability of your times, and the strength of salvation, the fear of the Lord is His treasure.

Isaiah 33:6

See then that you walk circumspectly, not as fools but as wise.
Ephesians 5:15

A Plea For Our Children

I want to take a moment and share what was in my spirit as I was writing the 105th prayer.

Our children are under attack by those wanting to remove their identity as a boy or girl. Our children's identity of who they are and who God has called them to be is under attack. To purpose of this attack is to try and make them feel lost, not knowing who they really are.

The devil wants to destroy and blind the children of what God has created them to be. So I pray against every demonic deception against our children's true identity. Our children are made in the image and likeness of God. I pray that our children's identities are restored. We take authority against the influences of this world trying to destroy our children's identity. We speak that the identity of the son of God is made known to our children.

We cancel all the attacks over our children's identity. We break the strongholds of their souls meant to bring confusion and a false identity to our children. Lord, we speak the Blood of Jesus over our children and grandchildren. We call them free from every false knowledge of who they are. We speak wholeness to our children's identity. We speak a healthy identity over our children, grandchildren, and the coming generations in Jesus' Name.

Please take one minute to pray in the Spirit to seal this prayer for our kids. Then we say "Amen," in agreement that it is done.

Release Of Abundant Life - Prayer 106

Today I pray the abundant life over our children. We speak a prosperous life of spiritual wholeness and great success. We call our children overcomers in this life, defeating every curse of poverty or lack by the Blood of Jesus.

We stop every spirit that is sent to kill, steal, or destroy our children. We declare the favor of God's grace over our children, causing them to have favor to succeed in every area of life. We call them blessed as they come in or go out of their regions. We speak great spiritual and earthly authority to arise upon our children that they may lead and take all that is in the enemie's hands.

Bring it into the hands of Your people so they can rule and reign in this life, being the head and not the tail. We speak great provision to come upon our children to live a peaceful and prosperous life. Our children are children of righteousness. Through Christ's righteousness our children will reign in life.

I call forth the mercy of God upon our children, delivering them from a hard and difficult life. Father God, give our children wisdom from above that makes them wise in this world. Thank You for covering our children and blessing them with all spiritual blessings. Make them rich inYou Lord, and help them to put Your Kingdom first in Jesus' Name.

Now let's take one minute to pray in the Spirit to seal this prayer for our kids. Then we say "Amen," in agreement that it is done.

Drawn By The Holy Spirit - Prayer 108

Today I pray that the Holy Spirit, our Helper and Comforter will be our children's Help. The Third Person of the Trinity that is the force at creation, the One that moved upon the face of the earth and brought order. We trust you Holy Spirit to move upon our children and bring them into order with their Creator.

Just as You moved upon this earth to separate light from darkness, Holy Spirit, move upon our children and separate them from darkness and bring them into the light.

Holy Spirit, just as you fell upon men and moved upon whole assemblies, move and fall upon our children. Our children need you Holy Spirit, to be set free and to come into the truth.

Holy Spirit, You are the power that draws all men unto the Father. Draw our children unto You and bring them to repentance. Holy Spirit, only You can fill our children saved and unsaved with spiritual wisdom, knowledge ,and understanding. Holy Spirit, Your anointing can heal their hearts and set them free from their captivities.

Let Your anointing fall on them and soften those whose hearts who have been hardened. Holy Spirit, teach them the ways of the Kingdom of righteousness, peace, and joy. Holy Spirit, fall upon their hearts with the love of God that they may know the Father's love and His forgiveness. Holy Spirit, Your anointing can free and deliver them from any demonic force controlling their souls. Holy Spirit cover, protect, lead, and enlighten them.

Bring them into the image of our Christ and remove the veil from their eyes. Thank you, Holy Spirit, for changing and blessing our children with Your presence and power.

Only you Holy Spirit, can bring them into their divine purpose and destiny.Holy Spirit, let Your peace be upon them and transform them into the sons of God.

Now let's take one minute to praise, worship, and pray in the Spirit to seal this prayer for our kids. Then we say "Amen," in agreement that it is done.

WE HAVE ACCESS

Remember, we have access to all that the Father has, because we are heirs of the promises.

Now we're no longer living like slaves under the law, but we enjoy being God's very own sons and daughters! And because we're His, we can access everything our Father has—for we are heirs because of what God has done!

Galatians 4:7 TPT

The Supernatural Power Of God - Prayer 109

Today we pray that our kids will experience the supernatural power of God. God will release signs, wonders, and miracles upon this next generation. Miracles that will turn many to the Lord. We declare that the young and old children of the righteous supernaturally come forth into the Kingdom. Jesus reached the children whose parents cried out for Him to deliver their children.

I declare and proclaim over our children supernatural protection and deliverance. We break every demonic influence, stronghold, or infirmity off of our children. We release Your word unto our children, and Your word shall cover and bless them with all their inheritance that was given to them before they entered this world.

Just as you delivered Your children from Pharaoh's hand so shall you deliver our children. We call all our children, whether saved or unsaved to be supernaturally guarded and made free by the power of the Holy Ghost now. In Jesus' Name.

Those children who are sick with any infirmities, we loose from their infirmities of sickness. Those children bound by evil influence, we break those influences and controls now. Those children that are saved but spiritually dead and unable to see by the Spirit, we set them free from spiritual blindness. For those children bound by fear, anxiety, worry, or depression, we break it off them now.

Those children who have been deceived by religion, philosophy, or new age, we free them now. And those children who have made the riches of this world of money, fame, and false beauty their gods, we deliver them now in Jesus' Name. We release the supernatural power of God over our children now! In Jesus' Name.

Now let's take one minute to pray in the Spirit to seal this prayer for our kids. Then we say "Amen," in agreement that it is done.

Release Of Faith - Prayer 110

Lord, we believe our children are blessed of You. We walk by faith regarding our children and not by sight. We call those things that be not as if they are. Father, let the words of our mouth as parents speak only the word of God over our children.

We cancel every cursed word or negative word over our children. We root out every negative seed planted into our childrens' hearts or souls. We remove the weeds and we speak to the seeds of the word planted in them to arise. We call forth every prophetic word over our children to come forth.

We speak great grace bringing signs, wonders and miracles in behalf of our children. Let Your Blood cleanse their minds from an evil conscience. We declare transformed children of God. That they come into Your glorious plan and purpose for their lives.

Now let's take one minute to pray in the Spirit to seal this prayer for our kids. Then we say "Amen," in agreement that it is done.

> *He did not waver at the promise of God through unbelief, but was strengthened in faith, giving glory to God, and being fully convinced that what He had promised He was also able to perform. And therefore "IT WAS ACCOUNTED TO HIM FOR RIGHTEOUSNESS." Romans 4:20-22*

The Power Of God's Grace - Prayer 111

Lord, we stand as intercessors for our children. We come boldly to the throne of grace and mercy. We call upon grace to intervene with our children young and old in this world and those that serve the world. Devils have tried to take our children into their systems and cultures, but today we break the influence of this world's systems and false beliefs off of our children.

We break deception and ruling forces off of our children. We break foolishness and speak spiritual wisdom unto our children. We declare our children shall be children of righteousness, justice, honor , obedience. Our children shall walk in favor and be blessed with all spiritual blessing. Our children will seek first God's Kingdom, and not the kingdoms of this world.

Our children shall overcome in this world by their faith in God. Our children shall not go astray, and not be led by fears, wrong desires, or wrong beliefs. Our children shall fulfill their destiny with signs, wonders, and miracles. They shall not be defeated. They shall live the abundant life in Jesus' Name.

Now let's take one minute to pray in the Spirit to seal this prayer for our kids. Then we say "Amen," in agreement that it is done.

Gifts And Callings - Prayer 112

Lord, today I speak to the callings and giftings given to our children to awaken. We call them into their destiny and speak to it, "Arise, and come forth." Our children were destined for greatness and chosen for the Master's plan. I release dreams and visions unto our children, that they may see and come into union with God's plan for them and their future.

I break the spirit of blindness to the things of the Spirit off of our children. I remove the dullness of hearing from their ears. I break the stubbornness and pride stopping them from doing Your will Lord. I rebuke the Spirit of unbelief hindering them from serving You, God. I speak healing to their hearts from wounds that may be keeping them out of Your divine purpose, Lord. I stop and cut off every ungodly relationship hindering them from their call. I break false philosophies and wrong teachings from their souls. Speak to them Holy Spirit, and bring them to their callings.

Minister to them Holy Spirit, and transform them into the Father's will. I release angels unto them to protect them and keep everything away that is destructive, all that will hinder their destiny in You, Lord. I break every destructive plan of Satan to deceive them out of God's plan. I cancel it now in Jesus' Name.

Our children will be the generation that advances Your kingdom in the earth like never before. In Jesus' Name. The precious Blood of our Christ will cover them and break them free from a false identity. Our children shall inherit all the good of the land. They shall have great favor and they shall see the goodness of our God. AMEN.

Now let's take one minute to pray in the Spirit to seal this prayer for our kids. Then we say "Amen," in agreement that it is done.

Rise Up In Power - Prayer 113

We speak power to arise in our children, so that they would be witnesses of Christ. We speak dreams and vision unto them. Dreams that will help them to see what they cannot see in the natural. Visions that will speak of God's vision for this world and for all humanity. Visions that will show them God's desire for their lives.

We speak hearts of mercy upon them, and that they would have compassion for others. Help them to be appreciative and to be thankful. I declare the mercy that will help them to forgive and care about others more then themselves. Our children shall walk in the Light and not in darkness.

Their eyes will be opened to the lies of the enemy. Our children shall be free from every selfishness and irresponsible behaviors. We call forth spiritual wisdom of the Spirit unto our kids. Our children shall be awakened to the truth.

We release truth unto them that they would be free from every deception. Our children are blessed of the Lord, and they shall fulfill their destiny. They shall live a good and long satisfying life in the Name of our Lord. Amen.

Now let's take one minute to pray in the Spirit to seal this prayer for our kids. Then we say "Amen," in agreement that it is done.

Blessings And Promises - Prayer 114

Glory to God! We bless our children with His glory. We cover our children with the promises of God. We speak forth our covenant with God for our children. Our covenant in His Blood, that our children will be our inheritance of blessings.

We cover our children in the anointing, breaking strongholds off of their lives. Its is Your righteousness Lord, that will reign in their life bringing them into their sonship. You have sent unto our children the Holy Spirit as their Comforter, Advocate, and Helper. From our heavenly position with Christ, we speak from our place of authority, releasing Your amazing love of mercy and compassion over our children. Protect them from every evil wicked work.

We bless our children with the power of our prayers, knowing that whatever we ask when we pray it shall be done in Jesus' Name. Our children are mighty in God and they will eat the good of the land. Amen.

Now let's take one minute to pray in the Spirit to seal this prayer for our kids. Then we say "Amen," in agreement that it is done.

Agreement With God And One Another - Prayer 115

Lord, it is written that if two shall agree on earth as touching anything, then whatever they shall ask of the Father it shall be given unto them. Today I ask for healing of the heart, soul, and body of our children. We call them not just to be healed but whole, spiritually healed in their relationship with the Lord.

They are healed in their bodies, we call them whole. We rebuke the spirit of infirmity off of their hearts, souls, and bodies. We call them free from every generational curse.

They are redeemed by the Blood of the lamb. They have been transferred from every curse of infirmity into the Kingdom of our God. We cast off every demonic infirmity and disease, and we call every part of their bodies healed and whole. They are free from every mental and physical disorder now in Jesus' Name.

> Surely He has borne our griefs And carried our sorrows; Yet we esteemed Him stricken, Smitten by God, and afflicted. But He was wounded for our transgressions, He was bruised for our iniquities; The chastisement for our peace was upon Him, And by His stripes we are healed. Isaiah 53:4

So let the redeemed of the Lord say so. We break every pain off of our children wherever they may be suffering in their hearts, minds, or physical body. We release peace unto them now, and cast down every worry and spirit of fear. Thank You, Lord for hearing our prayers.

Now let's take one minute to pray in the Spirit to seal this prayer for our kids. Then we say "Amen," in agreement that it is done.

Crying Out For The Lost - Prayer 116

My heart cries out for children who are lost, those that have been hardened in their hearts. We cry out for those who have allowed unbelief into their souls, and for those who have caved to the temptations and the pleasures of this world.

We will never stop loving you and praying for you. We will not judge you or condemn you. But we will fight for your souls. As parents, we will always be there for you.

My God says, in your weaknesses He will extend His mercy and unconditional love. It is His goodness that will lead you to repentance. So I call you all back into your salvation and your destiny, predestined before the foundations of this world.

Lord, we break every demonic control off of our children's lives. We cover them in Your Blood and Your mercy as they lie in darkness. We awaken them to the truth and speak faith to arise in their hearts.

We free them from any addiction of drugs, alcohol, opioids, perversion, witchcraft, ungodly relationships, depression, and fears. We break the spirit of poverty, disrespect, rebellion and hate off of your lives. We call you free from false intellect, wisdom of man, love of money and an anti-Christ spirit. We speak grace to you that your eyes will be opened and the wisdom of God comes unto our children.

Our children are free, blessed, overcomers, healed and delivered in Jesus' Name.

Thank You, Holy Spirit for drawing our kids unto our heavenly Father and our Lord. We release angels unto them to protect and watch over them. We speak the abundant life of God unto them. Thank You, Father God for showing mercy unto our children. Amen.

Now let's take one minute to pray in the Spirit to seal this prayer for our kids. Then we say "Amen," in agreement that it is done.

Renewing Minds - Prayer 117

Father God, only You can renew the minds of our children. You can break the strongholds and disobedience within their minds. We speak the mind of Christ over them. We break the false identities off of their minds. Give them, Holy Spirit, thoughts of our Father's heart for their lives. We speak sound thoughts of peace in their minds.

We come against the thoughts of evil, unbelief, anxiety and fear. We call for their minds to be full of wisdom and spiritual understanding of the Holy Spirit. Healing power, flow through every part of their minds and make them whole in their minds in Jesus' Name.

We align their minds to God's order and his perfect will.

Thank you, Lord, for renewing the minds of our kids in Jesus' Name.

Now let's take one minute to pray in the Spirit to seal this prayer for our kids. Then we say "Amen," in agreement that it is done.

> And do not be conformed to this world, but be transformed by the renewing of your mind, that you may prove what is that good and acceptable and perfect will of God. Romans 12:2

Breaking Away From Childishness - Prayer 118

We call maturity to arise in this younger generation of today. We break the foolish spirit of arrogance, pride, and a unteachable spirit. Let our young men and women break away from childish behaviors, jealousy, revenge, pride and irresponsible actions. We call our young generation into being the leaders of this next generation. Leaders of Your kingdom and Ekklesia, as sons of maturity.

Father, pour out Your Spirit upon our young and let them hear what the Spirit is saying to them. Bring forth a movement among our young that will reach their generation. Give them favor and opportunity to bring change into this world. Let Your righteous cause rise in this young generation.

We prophesy over them to arise as the watchman of their generation. Bring them into their true identity and remove all spots, wrinkles and blemishes of this world from their hearts.

We call them out of this world's systems into heaven's world as kings and priests. Anoint them to be the movers and shakers of their generation and this cosmos world. Fill them with Your Holy Spirit, and lead them as sons of God delivering this world from its corruption.

Now let's take one minute to pray in the Spirit to seal this prayer for our kids. Then we say "Amen," in agreement that it is done.

Weeping For Our Children - Prayer 119

My heart is weeping today because of those in the womb who are being tortured until they are dead. My heart is weeping for those sons and daughters of depression who want to commit suicide. My heart weeps for those who are homeless running from their pain. My heart weeps for those addicted to drugs or alcohol not knowing how to get free. My heart weeps for those incarcerated with no family or someone to love them.

My heart weeps for those whose homes were broken up by divorce or tragedy. My heart weeps for those who lost their parents to a tragic death. God, I cry out for mercy and grace. Deliver these children still in the womb. Bring help, Father to those who are in need of Your help from the heavy oppression they are going through.

God, reach this generation of hurting young people and children. Give us, the church—Your Ekklesia the wisdom and provision to help children and young adults all over the world. Forgive us fathers, as a nation, as leaders, and as parents.

We declare this generation will arise out of this world's systems. That our children will see the light, and You Father, will help them to be restored to their true destiny and identity. We as the church, travail for our children as we cover them with prayer, hope, love, and peace. We rebuke every spirit of fear and anxiety off of our children.

We call this next generation blessed, and ask that You would bring to them the riches of Your grace, Lord. In the Name above every

Name, Jesus.

Now let's take one minute to pray in the Spirit to seal this prayer for our kids. Then we say "Amen," in agreement that it is done.

Interceding For The Parents - Prayer 120

This is the last prayer of the 120 that the Lord asked me to pray. This prayer is for the parents. Father, I lift up every parent or grandparent. Lord, I ask You to bless all the parents that have done the best they knew how to do in raising their kids. Remove all guilt, condemnation of past mistakes and poor decisions made by us parents. Free the parents. Lord, to be there for their children. Give us parents greater wisdom in leading, helpin,or guiding our children.

We ask on behalf of the parents who have been rejected and held unforgiven of their mistakes, please Father, bring restoration and healing between parents and children. Restore all that has been lost and heal the broken hearts. Restore trust and help the children who have been hurt to have a heart to forgive.

Help all parents with the fears, worries, and hopelessness that they may be experiencing. Give the parents a heart of mercy towards the children who have hurt them and caused so many painful experiences.

For every parent that has lost a child or they do not know where their child may be, Lord give them strength. Father, no one knows the sorrow a parent goes through with their children except You Father, because of what You went through with Your son who died for our sins.

Father, help us parents to never give up and help us to keep hope and faith alive for our children. Heal the families, Lord and make every home a home of love and forgiveness in Jesus' Name.

Now let's take one minute to pray in the Spirit to seal this prayer for

the parents. Then we say "Amen," in agreement that it is done. Amen.

❖ ❖ ❖

FINALLY, MY BRETHREN

Remember.

We live the Supernatural Life.

It's now so obvious! We're not the children of the slave woman; we're the supernatural sons of the freewoman—sons of grace!

Galatians 4:31 TPT

AFTERWORD

Thank you for joining me in the release of these 120 prayers for our children, grandchildren, and the coming generations of family.

Let's continue to take a minute out of every day to intentionally pray. We are impacting the world with the goodness of the Kingdom of God.

www.ingramcontent.com/pod-product-compliance
Lightning Source LLC
Chambersburg PA
CBHW020744100426
42735CB00037B/490